Let All God's Glory Through

Peter G. van Breemen, S.J.

D1468460

PAULIST PRESS
New York and Mahwah, N.J.

Imprimatur: John A. Privett, S.J.
Provincial of the California Province
Los Gatos, California
November 1, 1993

Library of Congress Cataloging-in-Publication Data

Van Breemen, Peter G.,   1927-
    Let all God's glory through / Peter G. van Breemen.
        p.   cm.
    Includes bibliographical references.
    ISBN 0-8091-3525-6 (pbk.)
    1. Spiritual life—Catholic Church. 2. Catholic Church—Doctrines. I. Title.
BX2350.2.V177   1995   94-34867
248.4'82—dc20   CIP

Published by Paulist Press
997 Macarthur Boulevard
Mahwah, New Jersey 07430

Printed and bound in the
United States of America

NA-3200

Contents

Preface

The link between faith and daily life consists mainly in transparency. The separation of the two troubles many Christians and impoverishes our world. It will be overcome in the measure that we let "all God's glory through."* The meditations in this book focus on various ways to make us more transparent for God's glory, and thus to render our lives more faith-filled and our faith more lively.

Convinced that it is nothing less than fair and just, I tried to use gender-inclusive language. I must admit, though, that despite this inner conviction, it was not easy to carry it through. I suppose there are two main reasons. The battle against the inherent bias of the English language toward the masculine gender may be more vexatious for someone with a foreign mother tongue. I also discovered in the process how ingrained the masculine orientation is in my religious thinking and speaking. That taught me a valuable lesson, worth the effort. I am aware and sorry that I did not always succeed in my attempt.

Obviously many experiences with a good number of people flow into these reflections, especially my close contacts with the Jesuit tertians during the past eight years in Berlin, Germany. The latter accounts for the more explicit use of Ignatian sources, which readers familiar with my previous books will notice.

It is impossible to mention all the people who contributed to these pages. Some of them I want to thank in a special way. With tireless dedication and great love Sister Mary Jean Meier, RSM put her considerable competence and her whole heart into the

1

preparation of this book. She was an indispensable help in many ways, and I am deeply grateful to her. I also want to thank Father Thomas P. Rausch, S.J., the rector of the Jesuit community at Loyola Marymount University; though we had never met before, he was a faithful ally and support. The community of the Daughters of Charity at St. Vincent Medical Center provided warm hospitality, conducive to the writing of these chapters; to them and to the administration of the hospital I express my sincere thanks.

Los Angeles, California
October 19, 1993

* The words are taken from Hopkins' poem "The Blessed Virgin Compared to the Air We Breathe."

I

UNDER THE GAZE OF GOD

1. Look at Me, O God, that I May Love You

A woman engaged in Marriage Encounter once shared with a small group, "When my husband looks at me, I am so much greater and richer than when I look at myself. I sense so much more potential in me." Then her husband added, "When I experience my wife's loving gaze, I feel a sense of inner growth which seems to be lacking if I just look at myself in the mirror."

That is not an uncommon experience. In fact, Jean Vanier characterized love as "revealing to someone his or her own beauty." There is profound insight in recognizing that we need someone else to help us discover our own beauty. St. Ignatius capitalizes on this when he suggests that we begin our prayer by pausing and pondering how God looks at us:

> A step or two away from the place where I will make my contemplation or meditation, I will stand for the length of an Our Father. I will raise my mind and think how God our Lord is looking at me, and other such thoughts. Then I will make an act of reverence or humility (Sp Ex 75).

How one actually shapes this brief ritual will be different with each person and open to one's own creativity and devotion.

There are many ways to revitalize the awareness of God's loving gaze. A little private liturgy in which both body and soul enter into actual prayer can be a great help in deepening the authenticity and stillness of our prayer. Such a rite will, among other things, help to reduce distractions. The gaze of God, full of love and affirmation, should invariably be at the heart of this small personal opening liturgy; also, a bodily heartfelt expression of reverence and respect should always be a part of it. That is the wisdom of St. Ignatius' suggestion.

Occasionally, it is helpful to spend a longer period of time just centering on the affectionate and loving gaze of God. Whatever surfaces—my joys and sorrows, successes and failures, dreams and plans, anxieties and desires—I quietly let come and go, entrusting all to God. The heart of this prayer is solely that God looks at me with love and delight, and rejoices in my being present. The words of the prophet Zephaniah may be applied unreservedly:

> Yahweh, your God, is in your midst, a mighty savior; He will rejoice over you with gladness, and renew you in his love. He will sing joyfully because of you, as one sings at festivals (3:17–18).

The prophet evokes the image of God dancing for joy (as the Jerusalem Bible actually translates it), dancing for joy because of us. Our prayer then is to relish this joyful love of God; to bask in the warmth of that love. We ask for the grace to be in the divine presence without fear, and yet with a profound sense of awe.

In Genesis 16, Sarai's maidservant, Hagar, is abused so much by her mistress that in desperation she runs away from her into the desert. Then, in very dramatic circumstances, Yahweh appears to her and promises a generous answer to all of her prayers. So Hagar then calls the Lord "God who sees," and jubilantly cries out, "I have seen the one who sees me." Our predicament may not be quite as extreme as was Hagar's, and we may not be able to see God as she did, but we can be certain that God sees us in our needs and in our good fortunes. For us, too, the Holy One is "God who sees."

In Psalm 80 we pray to God three times, like a refrain: "Let your face shine upon us and we shall be saved" (vv 4,8,20). There is no fear in these words, just a certainty that the gaze of God will bring us relief. Similarly, Psalm 33 expresses the faith-conviction that God wants us to *live*: "Yahweh looks on those who revere him, on those who hope in his love, to rescue their souls from death, to keep them alive in famine" (vv 18, 19). In Psalm 139 the life-giving gaze of God is portrayed even more intimately: "It was you who created my being, knit me together in my mother's womb. I thank you for the wonder of my being, for the wonders of all your creation. Already you knew my soul, my body held no secret from you when I was being fashioned in secret and molded in the depths of the earth" (vv 13–15).

These psalms, as well as many others, express a deep-seated knowledge which has grown in generations of praying people: that the look of God accomplishes divine goodness, and that it is wholesome to dwell under this gaze. Meditating on these psalms will help us overcome a negative fear of God which we might have imbibed and which is so hard to expel.

St. Augustine prays with stark confidence: *aspice me ut diligam te*; "look at me, that I may love you." He has no doubts about the serenity of God's gaze, and that it will bring out the best in us—the love of God.

Blessed Beatrice of Nazareth, (†1268) begs in one of her simple, but profound prayers:

> Teach me to pray, God.
> You see everything
> You hear everything
> You know everything
> You experience everything in me and with me,
> For you are my companion and my beloved.
> Nothing is hidden from you.
> Your love for me is light,
> And in this light you see everything.

Yes, God sees and knows all things, but always in the light of infinite love. How many people feel lonely, abandoned, ignored, not seen nor heard, and have no one with whom to share. Such irony, for at the same time someone "stands at the door and knocks";

someone who wants to enter and to share a meal (cf. Rev 3:20). That someone knows all about them in the kindly light of gentle love.

In 1835, John Henry Newman, then vicar of the Anglican parish of St. Mary the Virgin in Oxford, gave an outstanding and still famous homily on "A Particular Providence as Revealed in the Gospel." Toward the end of the sermon he says:

> God beholds you individually, whoever you are. He "calls you by your name." He sees you, and understands you, as He made you. He knows what is in you, all your own peculiar feelings and thoughts, your dispositions and likings, your strength and your weakness. He views you in your day of rejoicing, and your day of sorrow. He sympathizes in your hopes and your temptations. He interests Himself in all your anxieties and remembrances, all the risings and fallings of your spirit. He has numbered the very hairs of your head and the cubits of your stature. He compasses you round and bears you in His arms; He takes you up and sets you down. He notes your very countenance, whether smiling or in tears, whether healthful or sickly. He looks tenderly upon your hands and your feet; He hears your voice, the beating of your heart, and your very breathing. You do not love yourself better than He loves you.[1]

Spontaneously, I feel the urge to add to that last sentence that it is not at all difficult for God to love us more than we love ourselves. Most people really do not love themselves that much; they need constant affirmation from others as well as much coddling of themselves to make up for this lack of love. It would be a far greater help to realize how much God's loving gaze is always upon us.

God also knows all about our shadow, and that knowledge is assimilated into the loving gaze. In turn this can help us accept and integrate our shadow. To our surpise we will then discover, as C.G. Jung remarked, that it is 90 percent gold. Indeed, "Let your face shine on us and we shall be saved" (Ps 80).

Usually we are anxious about exposing ourselves to the risk of not being understood. This natural fear can lure us into playing a game which we hope will protect us, into hiding behind a mask which we believe gives us a certain security. The liberating message for us now is that we don't need a mask before God, because the Holy One already knows, understands, and accepts us. "Your love for me is light, and in this light you see everything." With God we can be unreservedly and completely honest. That is one of the graces of prayer—it need not be pious, but it *can* and *must* be honest. It is vital that in my prayer everything—the good, the bad, and the in-between is brought before God, is exposed to God's look. That honesty ensures wholeness.

When we are confused or uncertain, we can derive great comfort from knowing that someone "knows all about us," really seeing through us with absolute clarity, and that this someone never lets us down, but always in unshakable faithfulness supports us as we are (and not as we should be). When people overestimate us, we feel awkward and may get discouraged by a challenge beyond our capacity. On the other hand, when people underestimate us, we feel insulted and sense the urge to assert ourselves. How seldom are we estimated correctly!

When Dietrich Bonhoeffer was incarcerated in the infamous Nazi prison in Berlin-Tegel, he articulated this inner struggle in the form of a poem. Most letters and papers he wrote in prison express his profound and sometimes groundbreaking thinking. This very personal poem, however, reveals some of his innermost feelings. In its last line he intimated discreetly where he found his inner strength while enduring his painful trial.

WHO AM I?
Who am I? They often tell me
I step from my cell's confinement
calmly, cheerfully, firmly,
like a squire from his country-house.

Who am I? They often tell me
I talk to my warders
freely and friendly and clearly,
as though it were mine to command.

Who am I? They also tell me
I bear the days of misfortune
equably, smilingly, proudly,
like one accustomed to win.

Am I then really all that which other men tell of?
Or am I only what I know of myself,
restless and longing and sick, like a bird in a cage,
struggling for breath,
as though hands were compressing my throat,
yearning for colors, for flowers, for the voices of birds,
thirsting for words of kindness, for neighborliness,
trembling for rage because of arbitrariness and petty insults,
tossing in expectation of great events,
powerlessly trembling for friends at an infinite distance,
weary and empty at praying, at thinking, at making,
faint, and ready to say farewell to it all?

Who am I? This or the other?
Am I one person today, and tomorrow another?
Am I both at once? A hypocrite before others,
and before myself a contemptibly woebegone weakling?
Or is something within me still like a beaten army,
fleeing in disorder from victory already achieved?

Who am I? They mock me, these lonely questions of mine.
Whoever I am, thou knowest, O God, I am thine.[2]

God's loving gaze gives us not only a sense of genuine self-worth, it also creates in us a secure feeling. Time and time again this security allows us to cross new borders into an ever more developing and richer life. The all-encompassing gaze of God enhances our gifts and strengthens our abilities which otherwise would remain dormant.

Our most inspiring example is Jesus himself. The security which he experienced in the unity with his Father rendered him extremely open. It enabled him to relate lovingly with others, also at times to disagree with them (and then to hold his ground in a fair conflict). All his encounters were intended to bring out the best in others.

God's gaze is creative in the strictest sense of the word. So Romano Guardini prays:

> Continually I receive myself from your hand.
> That is my truth and my joy.
> Continually your eye looks at me
> And I live on your look,
> You, my creator and my salvation.
> Teach me, in the silence of your presence,
> To grasp the mystery that I am.
> And that I am through you and before you and for you.[3]

It is in God's look that we meet love: *God's* love which loved us into being; and *our* love which God wants to enkindle ever more as the fulfillment of our lives. What the Old Testament says about the covenant between Yahweh and the chosen people, the New Testament extends to every individual person. We may all apply it to ourselves in a very personal way. Let Ezekiel be an example: "I saw you as I was passing. Your time had come, the time for love" (16:8, *JB*); and Song of Songs, "I am my Beloved's, and his desire is for me" (7:11, *JB*). At the beginning of a retreat, retreatants have sometimes spent several hours and even several days, just with the second part of the last verse. To open oneself in faith to these words, to take them very personally, leads us to a breadth and depth which is fulfilling and liberating. Another well-known example is Hosea's text where Yahweh says, "So I will allure her; I will lead her into the desert and speak to her heart" (2:16). The word allure means "to do everything possible to arouse the other person's love, but without coercing." *God* wants to obtain *our* love! We are precious and treasured in God's eyes. We mean so very, very much to God.

The Holy One uses no violence since true love can never be forced, but God does everything possible to express the divine love and to call forth ours. "I will espouse you to me forever: I will espouse you in right and in justice, in love and in mercy; I will espouse you in fidelity, and you shall know the Lord" (Hos 2:21–22). The covenant which God desires and offers us is portrayed in images of great intimacy.

Jesus makes visible how God looks. Looking at the rich young man, Jesus loved him (Mk 10:21). The sinful woman knew before Jesus said a single word to her, just by his eyes, that he did not condemn her and that she could take off her mask before him, which she then did with abandon (Lk 7:36–50). When Jesus asked the woman caught in adultery whether no one had condemned her, and then added, "Neither do I condemn you," she must have beheld in his eyes heaven itself (Jn 8:1–11). The look of Jesus can also trigger contrition. Judas, alas, made himself impervious to this gaze; Peter found his salvation in it. "The Lord turned and looked at Peter; and Peter remembered the words of the Lord, how he had said to him, 'Before the cock crows today, you will deny me three times.' He went out and began to weep bitterly" (Lk 22:61–62).

An astute commentary on this last quotation by the late and unforgettable Anthony de Mello, S.J., concludes this chapter:

I had a fairly good relationship with the Lord. I would ask him for things, converse with him, praise him, thank him....

But always I had this uncomfortable feeling that he wanted me to look into his eyes...And I would not. I would talk but look away when I sensed he was looking at me.

I always looked away. And I knew why. I was afraid. I thought I should find an accusation there of some unrepented sin. I thought I should find a demand there: there would be something he wanted from me.

One day I finally summoned up courage and looked! There was no accusation. There was no demand. The eyes just said. "I love you." I looked long into those eyes. I looked searchingly. Still, the only message was, "I love you!"

And I walked out and, like Peter, I wept.[4]

II

COPING WITH EVIL

2. God at a Distance

Anthony de Mello's story strikes a chord in most people's hearts, because it articulates so tersely what we all feel. We experience a deep longing for true intimacy with God and pray with St. Augustine, "Restless is our heart, until it finds rest in you." Each of us yearns to be loved unconditionally; and, God is love—precisely that unconditional love which our hearts crave.

But there is also the opposite tendency; we are afraid of God and avoid the risk of getting too close. Rather than being truly intimate, we tend to restrict ourselves to "a fairly good relationship." We make ourselves believe, "That will do." How many devout people keep God at arm's length. Somehow we strike a balance between our longing for and our aversion to God. "We ask him for things, converse with him, praise him, thank him"...and keep our distance. We long for God's love, yet run away from it, because it isn't easy to let ourselves be really loved in such a limitless way. We seek and we flee at the same time!

Both movements, though, are not operative in the same degree of consciousness. I assume that with most readers of these pages, the movement *away from* God is rather hidden, repressed, and mostly subconscious; whereas the movement *toward* God is much more deliberate and cultivated. With many people, this ratio might be inverse; but if so, they would not likely pick up a book such as this one. The opposite of love is not so much hatred, but rather indifference. It is precisely in this apathy that the resistance of all of us against God ensconces itself.

Even good Christians often arrange their lives in such a manner that, in fact, God plays only a limited role in them. Undoubtedly, many are not aware of this, and would be shocked if they could realistically see through their own behavior. We may think of ourselves as devout people, speak often about God (or perhaps not!), participate in religious activities, volunteer our services where needed, take time for prayer and even attend daily mass. However, our lives are far more dominated by a flight from God than we are ready to admit. Although our lives may be brimming with the spiritual, yet we have little room for God. What is so unfortunate is that we are not conscious of how our religious busyness serves as an avoidance of God. With our pious activities we build a very effective defense system against the unconditional love of God which, as we intuitively sense, will lead eventually to our complete surrender. Religion can thus become a levee against God.[1]

If we are genuinely to allow God into our lives, to let God truly be God, many of our thoughts and actions must change. Without admitting this explicitly (and perhaps even while stressing the exact opposite), we may not be ready for this change. So, with all our piety, we keep God at a safe distance. The closer we draw to God, the more we discover what a massive barricade we erect to hide from the Holy One. We cling to our activities, relationships, career, reputation, convictions, looks, and health. We find our security and self-worth in these things and become entrenched in them. We lose our inner freedom to truly let God be God, and to make God's kingdom our first priority.

Repent

Jesus in his ministry attacked this attitude head on. The first words he speaks in Mark's gospel are: "This is the time of fulfillment. The kingdom of God is at hand. Repent, and believe in the Good News" (1:15). Overall this message is certainly encouraging; however, the terse word "repent" in the middle of it, is less palatable, since it calls so bluntly for a profound change of heart and conduct. Someone might try to explain it away by reasoning that this was precisely the very beginning of Jesus' preaching, and everyone knows that beginners tend to make mistakes. However, the fact of the matter is, that throughout his public life, Jesus stressed the need for repentance again and again. He made it a recurring theme. Repentance is and remains the first demand of the gospel, not just chronologically.

If, for instance, we take Luke's gospel, we find him relating that the people came to Jesus very upset because Pilate had ordered the death of some Galileans and mingled their blood with that of the animals they wanted to sacrifice. For the Jews, blood is sacred since it is the carrier of life (cf. Lev 17:14). The book of Leviticus gives detailed regulations which prescribe how to deal with blood. To them in their sensitivity, the mingling of human, not to mention, Jewish blood with that of animals was a shocking sacrilege. The people who came to Jesus in their anger probably thought that this was the last straw and that the time for a revolution against the Romans had come. Jesus reacted differently. He did call for a revolution, not, however against the foreign rule of the Romans, but against the foreign rule of the evil in each person. That was, and is, a much more radical revolution. "Do you think that because these Galileans suffered in this way they were greater sinners than all other Galileans? By no means! But I tell you, if you do not repent, you will all perish as they did!" (Lk 13:2–3). Then Jesus adds, "Or those eighteen people who were killed when the tower at Siloam fell on them—do you think they were more guilty than everyone else who lived in Jerusalem? By no means! But I tell you, if you do not repent, you will all perish as they did!" (Lk 13:4–5).

The comforting parable of the barren fig tree in the orchard follows in Luke's sequence. The gardener pleads for his fruitless tree: "Sir, leave it for one more year, and I shall cultivate the ground around it and fertilize it; it may bear fruit in the future." But notwithstanding his tender care, he cannot help but add, "If not, you can cut it down" (Lk 13:6–9).

Luke next records in his subtle composition, the cure of a woman crippled for eighteen years and completely bent over. The principal message of this passage is that the sabbath was made for the people, not the people for the sabbath, and that the Son of man is lord of the sabbath. It is relevant, though, that the Son of man breaks through the narrow-minded and uncharitable interpretation of the sabbath by working precisely this particular healing. The woman bent double for so many years had lived in a confined world which left her no perspective. She could see only her feet. To other people she was inferior, barely capable of eye contact, and she was always the one who had to try laboriously to look up—not to speak of the physical pain she had been enduring throughout those eighteen years. Tradition soon interpreted her predicament as an image of sin—the stooped person, bound and bent around self.[2] Repentance then means, and that is Luke's discreet message in this context, to restore a person's uprightness and human dignity. Luke thus points out the liberating and fulfilling aspects of repentance in an appealing, eloquent way.

This threefold sequence in Luke's gospel is by no means the only passage which accentuates repentance, or *metanoia*, as it is called in Greek. As Jesus enters Jerusalem on Palm Sunday amidst the jubilant acclaim of the crowds, he suddenly begins to cry over the city, because it "does not know what makes for peace." (Lk 19:41–44). Five days later, as Jesus was carrying his cross, he was led out of the city to Golgotha to complete his passion "outside the gate" (Heb 13:12). On his way he told the women not to mourn for him but for themselves and their children, and again called them to repentance (Lk 23:27–31). With a stirring appeal for metanoia, Jesus entered the city at the beginning of Holy Week; on the day of his death, he left the city with a similar plea. If a meditation on the way of the cross does not challenge our own way of life and move us toward repentance, then our piety is too sweet and lacking in commitment. To delve wholeheartedly into the memory of Jesus is a risky adventure!

Just before his ascension the risen Jesus missions his disciples for the last time. Once more the theme of repentance is at the heart of his message: "Thus it is written that the Messiah would suffer and rise from the dead on the third day and that repentance for the forgiveness of sins, would be preached in his name to all the nations, beginning from Jerusalem" (Lk 24:46–47).

In the Acts of the Apostles there are several major apostolic discourses of Peter and Paul. The close of each of these is invariably a call to repentance to obtain the forgiveness of sins. This fact demonstrates how seriously the apostles took the final mission of Jesus.

Paul writes in his letter to the Romans, "Do your hold God's priceless kindness, forbearance, and patience in low esteem, unaware that the kindness of God would lead you to repentance?" (2:4). It is God's kindness, not God's wrath, that leads us to repentance, for metanoia is not a punishment or a stripping away; rather it is a coming to life, an unfolding and enhancing of one's dignity and self-worth as the healing of the crippled woman expressed so powerfully. It is in Jesus that God's kindness leads us indeed to repentance. That is what Jesus is all about.

Our spontaneous negative reaction to metanoia is only the tip of the iceberg. Our resistance is deeply ingrained and usually it takes a long time to overcome it. Slowly we have to interiorize the liberating power of biblical repentance.

3. Metanoia

There are numerous quotations in scripture that can nourish our reflection on metanoia, for it is indeed a key word of the good news which is repeated again and again. But there are also numerous defense mechanisms in us which counteract and attempt to dilute the biblical appeal. For instance, try to picture metanoia as a once-in-a-lifetime experience which we have put behind us long ago; or, as something vitally important...for others! Such escapes are not at all rare. Sometimes one gets the impression that the most unambiguous common belief that conservatives and liberals share is the holy conviction that it is the other who has to repent. So many discussions boil down to the statement that the other person or group should reform, which seems to be a rather meager basis for fruitful cooperation in building church. A proverb in East Africa says: "Evil is like a hill; each one stands on his and points to the other one." How often do we ourselves choose from an abundant variety of theological and spiritual articles and lectures exactly those which confirm and reassure us in our way of thinking and in no way challenge us to a real conversion. Rabbi Bunam was right when he remarked, "The great human guilt is not the sins we commit; after all, the temptation is so strong and our strength so little. *The great guilt is that we can come to repentance any moment, and do not do it.*" In the past, an unhealthy spirituality has sometimes talked people into inauthentic guilt feelings, and in doing so, caused much pain and harm. Yet the repression of guilt and of our need for metanoia seems to be the greater danger today, and may bring even more misery into the world than did the fire and brimstone sermon of old.

Repentance undoubtedly demands sacrifices of us. However, we must not overlook the fact that by turning a deaf ear to repentance, we often give rise to far greater distress than the metanoia would cause us. At times we inflict incredible pressure on ourselves just to avoid our necessary and liberating conversion. In fact, by turning our back on metanoia, we inflict much unnecessary pain and suffering on ourselves and on others. Metanoia does *not* mean a stifling of our personality; on the contrary! Metanoia means letting our identity reach its full unfolding in the strength of the gospel. It helps us finally to overcome our own timidity and truly become the person we are meant to be by tapping into the source of life itself. God does not want us to hold back but is glorified by our bearing much fruit (Jn 15:8), by a truly worthwhile life. God, who thinks so much more of us than we do of ourselves, wants our most precious gifts to shine forth (cf. Mt 5:14–16). Our creator called us into existence with an immense desire and love. There is nothing halfhearted about that. Repentance is the means of generating a new sense of greatness and self-worth in us, not to mention the positive affects it has on the family and the community—greater understanding, forgiveness, gentleness, and encouragement.

Love has many names; metanoia is one of them.

The Topography of Metanoia

In the landscape of our personality, conversion can be sketched in three layers:

First, there is the inner core of our being. Two quotations from Genesis characterize this: the phrase repeated on four days, "God saw how good it was" (on the second day of creation this word is lacking!), and the word of the sixth day: "God looked at everything he had made, and found it very good" (Gn 1: 4ff, 31). This inner core is the place where we keep the word of Jesus; therefore, it is where he and the Father make their dwelling (cf Jn 14:23). It is the pinnacle of the soul[1] where God is to us Father and Mother, where God's love meets no hindrance, and where we, according to Jesus' request, should remain (cf. Jn 15:9). In this inner core of our being, the kingdom of God is within us (cf. Lk 17:21). Peace and a fruitful stillness reign here.

Second, this kernel is surrounded by a zone of thorns and thistles, of sweat and pain, of emptiness and loneliness. In this layer boredom and meaninglessness, anger and anguish, misunderstanding and being misunderstood hold sway. It is the realm of guilt, bitterness, and hatred.

Third, on top of this layer human nature builds a protective shield to ward off pain and distress. This zone is heavily cushioned with riches and consumption, with career and profit, with honor and prestige. Often a good deal of religion is built into this sheltering cover. Over-activity, hard liquor, and drugs can also be a part of it. In fact, most of the elements of this third zone are ambivalent; they can just as well lead us to our true self and to God, as they can shield us from them. It is the realm of the ambiguity—neither hot nor cold, neither a wholehearted yes nor a resolute no. Some people deliberately live only in this third zone.

Metanoia is to undertake the journey from this superficial layer into the inner core. We all know that this is the longest journey a person can make. After the initial joy of having finally made up one's mind to do this, the road soon leads into the zone of pain and distress. A strong determination not to shirk suffering (just as Jesus did not recoil from the passion when it turned out to be an essential part of his mission), is necessary if one is to reach the inner kernel. There can be no true conversion nor true redemption without a willingness to suffer. Jesus said to his disciples, "Whoever wishes to come after me must deny him or her self, take up his cross, and follow me. For whoever wishes to save his or her life, will lose it, but whoever loses his or her life for my sake will find it" (Mt 16:24–25). However, the cross in our life is fruitful only if we accept it. If we don't, it creates a sense of discontent, self-pity, and oftentimes bitterness. That is why the words of the last supper, repeated in each mass, are so meaningful. "This is my body, which will be *given up* for you." Whoever takes up his cross in this way, follows Jesus into the realm, where he lives in us, where we, too, are one with the Father and where the source of life gushes forth. Then our affectivity—that precious talent which God has laid in our hearts—can be tuned so that instinctively we are attracted to all that is good and shy away from what is evil.

What Then Is Metanoia?

Biblical theology tells us that metanoia is a deep change of heart and thinking; a complete reorientation toward God which results in a new pattern of actions and reactions. It is our total surrender to God with a firm determination to fulfill God's will in all things.

But, now, let us make this description more practical. Every day we make many decisions. Most of them are small; occasionally there is a more important one; and, once in a great while, a major decision. The many small choices are, nevertheless, significant since taken together they determine our life-style which expresses our basic stance far more than our words and actions do. In our life-style our underlying integrity is at stake. It must be added, though, that much in our lives is not of our own choice; we are simply not capable of changing it. Yet, even in these cases it still depends on us how we react to the inevitable. That choice always remains ours. Moreover, we often act in a certain routine manner or in a spontaneous, impulsive way so that many choices are not truly deliberate.

However, in whatever way they are reached, decisions are important in life. St. Augustine compares them with the strings of a harp; a frame is indispensable, yet it is the strings that make the music. John C. Haughey, S.J., makes the point more colorfully:

> Not withstanding all the appearances to the contrary, an individual does not become a person by growing upward physically, outward spacially, or inward reflectively. Selfhood comes to be primarily by choosing. In the act of choosing, most of all, the spirit of a person stands forth and is enfleshed. Our choices express our self-understanding and at the same time make self-understanding possible.

By contrast, non-choosers and half-choosers live in the immature condition of wanting to "play everything by ear." They dance when another pipes, and wail when another determines that a dirge is called for. An individual who is insufficiently self-determining will find that his milieu, his family, his appetites, or any other force external to himself, usurp the place and function his own spirit should assume. Men have battled for centuries against slavery in the firm belief that its involuntary form of determinism is evil. The irony of our present age is that so many people, though free to do otherwise, allow themselves to become afflicted with the voluntary slavery of indetermination.[2]

Now, the point is, that all our decisions, small or large, deliberate or tacit, are made according to a set of priorities which we have interiorized. Whenever we have an option, it is by checking the ranking of our values (no matter how implicitly we do this checking) that we decide. Any change in the scale of our priorities will immediately lead to different decisions and consequently to a different life-style. If it does not come across as disrespectful, we could compare it with a computer program in which even the slightest change will immediately modify the output.

Metanoia, then, is an overhaul of our priorities. A car, or any other delicate instrument, requires regular checkups. All the more an occasional tuning is required for our conscience, that "still quiet voice within" that regulates our entire life. Over the years our priorities shift without our even noticing it. We may honestly believe that certain values have a high priority in our life, while in fact they have slipped down considerably; yet we think that they still rank high. Similarly, we may believe that certain values do not mean much to us, yet imperceptibly they have taken over much of our way of choosing and acting. Whoever has not gone into this matter carefully for some time will be in for some big, and probably unpleasant, surprises.

False priorities shield us from the love and will of God; they are all the more effective the less conscious we are of them. They build in us that defense mechanism through which the word of God can hardly penetrate. The heart of sin is that we do not let ourselves be loved by God; in other words, since God *is* love, that we do not let God be God. Normally, this refusal to let God be God, be love, does not happen explicitly, but through our life-style, which in turn is determined by the order of our priorities. Metanoia, then, is to face this order and to correct it. This may seem harmless, yet it tackles basic behavioral patterns which we may experience as gratifying and may rationalize to a great extent.

It is to this metanoia that Jesus consistently calls us. He makes it the condition for our faith in him, for becoming his disciple.

4. To Live on Forgiveness

How Do We Come to Repentance?

The call to repent can grip us at any moment, because "indeed, the word of God is living and effective, sharper than any two-edged sword penetrating even between soul and spirit, joints and marrow, and able to discern reflections and thoughts of the heart" (Heb 4:12). Ordinarily, however, God's word, especially his appeal to metanoia, touches us to the degree that our hearts are open. A feeling of discontent or an inner hunger can enhance the openness of our hearts. We sense that something is not right. We experience an uneasiness and distress which are quite corrosive, sapping our energy and joy, yet we can't put a finger on them. If we are honest, we have to admit that really nothing is lacking—except happiness. We have a thousand reasons to be content, and yet we are not.

What we experience is not the grief one suffers over a loss, but rather a vague depression so ingrained that nothing worthwhile can rouse our interest. The soul feels paralyzed, bored, discouraged. All joy has evaporated; all vigor is gone. It does not take a great deal of honesty to realize that the cause of all this lies not in the external circumstances, but within oneself. The easy way out is to refuse to face the situation and to escape by eating, sleeping, chatting, drinking, watching television, or overactivity. Today what is commonly blamed as consumerism, is often a symptom of this deep-seated unhappiness. Our bogus priorities block the access to our heart. Only when we face our life with courage and sincerity can we identify and tackle the real problem. A good question would be, "What keeps me from living with all my heart as I really want to live?" Or, an even more basic question, "What do I really want?"

The first word Jesus speakes in John's gospel is precisely this question, "What are you looking for?" (1:38) Again, at the end of his gospel the same pertinent question, slightly modified, recurs, "Whom are you looking for?" (20:15) This is *the* question of the Johannine Jesus. The fourth gospel is encapsuled in this vital question: what are our most genuine desires? They are taken very, very seriously. The good news is that our sincerest desires are precisely what God wants. Our being truly ourselves is exactly God's will. Selfhood is sacred, since God is the Deepest Ground of our being. In the core of our personality there is no opposition between God and us; that tension arises only on the surface, insofar as we drift away from our authentic self. When we dodge the question of what we most deeply yearn for, we inevitably start searching out things which we do not really want.

Three questions, which are basically one and the same, may help us to zero in on this vital question:

1. To what extent does egotism dominate our life? This is not meant in the sense of gross selfishness, but rather of a subtle self-seeking in all we do. Externally, our actions and motivations appear very noble and forthright (we make sure of that!); but, deep down in our hearts, we know that we are always seeking our own advantage. The service we give is more a coveting of recognition and affection than an expression of love.

2. How great is our inability to really love the other? There are times when we truly succeed in loving genuinely. But then we take back what we had previously given. We turn in on ourselves. Our ego takes center stage, and the others are reduced to satellites spinning around the center of our ego. And we know it!

3. Behind our inability to love, is there perhaps a rejection of certain people? We may be able to play with them, but in our heart of hearts (so deep, that we do not dare let it surface), we consider the other person as a burden or a threat. We would prefer a world without this person; or—in our more generous moments—we may allow this person to live; but then, please, on another continent.

However, because this feeling is too paltry to be admitted, it is repressed and then manifests itself as anxiety and dislike.

The Wonder of Forgiveness

If in any way we delve seriously into the basic question, we cannot get around the recognition of our own guilt. That is hard. It is next to impossible to face one's guilt, if one is uncertain about being accepted and loved after having owned up to it. Or, to state it in another way, a person who cannot admit guilt is an insecure person. One of the secrets of Jesus was that he always created an atmosphere of unconditional acceptance, an atmosphere in which guilt could be faced. In this freeing attitude, more than anywhere else, he was the true image of his Abba, the perfect copy of God's nature (cf. Heb 1:3). By this liberating behavior he also lived up to his own name as interpreted by Matthew: "He will save his people from their sins" (1:21).[1]

Let us adapt the story of Zacchaeus to our everyday way of life so as to grasp how extraordinary Jesus' approach really is.[2] Zacchaeus was a chief tax collector in Jericho. He made his fortune as a collaborator with the hated Roman occupiers. It was obvious that he was guilty of treason, entirely at the cost of his own people and very much to his own profit.

Now this man wanted to see Jesus. But, thank God, Jesus was enough of a prophet to see through the trap. When Zacchaeus made his request, Jesus rebuked him openly and sharply, "How do you, a tax collector and traitor dare to invite me, the prophet!" However, Jesus agreed to consider his request provided this twofold condition was met: you must give fourfold restitution for every extortion; and, you must give half of all you possess to the poor. Jesus added, "Unless you fulfill these stipulations, you are not worthy to receive me." After Zacchaeus had complied with the conditions, Jesus went to visit him in his house.

Perhaps this revised version of the story does not seem strange to us. Maybe it is the way a request would be handled in our world. By the same token though, it becomes clear how very unusual Jesus' attitude was, and still is. His love is always unconditional; it is precisely because he accepts others unreservedly as they are, that he enables them to change freely.

The Pharisees spread the opposite spirit. Their demeanor was that of self-righteousness, of judging and condemning others. This certainly was not an encouragement to acknowledge faults; on the contrary, it fostered repression. What is repressed, however, keeps exerting pressure, but in an obscure, subconscious way. Repression can never be a lasting solution; it smacks of untruthfulness and hypocrisy.

The contrast between the attitudes of Jesus and the Pharisees comes out clearly in the gospel story of the sinful woman who came to Jesus while he was the dinner guest of Simon, the Pharisee (Lk 7:36–50). Branded and spurned as a sinful woman, she sought protection in her withdrawal behind a sturdy mask. Even before Jesus had said a word to her, she knows that *he* accepts her. His eyes, his whole being convey that message unmistakably. She knows intuitively that he accepts her despite her sinfulness. Before Jesus she needs no mask; she can cry and give free reign to her pain and her love. His as yet unspoken forgiveness has released her affection. It is not her love which earns her forgiveness; on the contrary, her great love is the fruit of her being forgiven.

Simon, the host, is a privileged witness to this moving transformation, yet he is unable to enter into her profound change and holds stubbornly to his condemnation of the woman. Jesus then uses a parable to point out to Simon that the one who is pardoned more will, as a consequence, love more.

Not only the *confession* of guilt, but even the *awareness* of it hinges on the inner certainty that one is truly loved, even with one's guilt. Only people who know that they are completely and genuinely loved, can really experience full-fledged guilt. After all, guilt is precisely the abuse of this love. But it is only when we believe, or at least have a hunch, that this love is greater than our guilt could ever be, that we can courageously face it.

Yet, even in such favorable circumstances, a great part of our guilt remains hidden from our consciousness. Ninety percent of an iceberg is always under water. That is a law of nature based on the specific gravity of ice. Similarly, a large proportion of our guilt always remains subconscious. We are not asked to lift the iceberg of our guilt out of the water. It is sufficient that we honestly observe what already floats by itself above the waterline of our consciousness. Have we not all experienced in our sincere confessions that we are not able to articulate fully all our guilt? That corresponds to the nature of it.

The Christian tradition throughout the centuries has emphasized a vital grace in which a person experiences a heartfelt awareness of being a veritable sinner, and *at the same time* truly loved by God. This grace is rarer than one would hope. There are many people who are very aware of their guilt and their moral failures; but for most of them the knowledge that they are, nevertheless, truly loved by God is lacking to a large extent. On the other hand, there are fortunately many people who know in their hearts that they are really and fully loved by God and live on that; but then again many of these may confess with their lips that they are sinners, yet in their heart of hearts this is hardly a living conviction. When they pray for the conversion of sinners, they spontaneously think of others. People who hold fast to both realities simultaneously, personally and unreservedly loved by God while concurrently sinful in the full sense of the word—are rare.

In the Spiritual Exercises of St. Ignatius, this grace of intimate recognition of being a sinner loved by God is the fruit of what he calls the "first week." This grace is so vital for the retreat that Ignatius did not want to proceed further when it seemed lacking. It is insufficient for beginning the second week, if the retreatants repent and confess their sins with the tacit impression that the sinfulness is hereby overcome. The genuine grace of this phase of the Exercises is a knowledge of the heart that our sins are forgiven, that we remain sinful people, and that we as such, nevertheless, really are loved by God. When in 1974/75 the Society of Jesus, in its most representative body (namely, its General Congregation, in this case the 32nd), asked itself just what it means to be a Jesuit, the answer began with the words: "It is to know that one is a sinner, yet called to be a companion of Jesus as Ignatius was." That statement articulates concisely the grace of the first week.

Verse 4 of Psalm 130 can be translated as: "With you is forgiveness and on this we live." Absolution is not an unrepeated occurrence. We live steadily on forgiveness. When it is omitted in our diet for any length of time, we become ill in the same way as when certain vitamins are lacking for too long. To live on forgiveness is a vital Christian art. Whoever has mastered this art finds forgiveness continuously and in many different forms, all of which culminate in the sacrament of reconciliation. The one who has found the personal approach to this sacrament will also in everyday life seek and find reconciliation. The person who daily lives on forgiveness will regularly receive God's remission in a sacramental way. The one action complements and strengthens the other.

Forgiveness has to be both given and received. We cannot produce it ourselves. That is a basic truism in the gospels: no one can forgive sins but God alone. We touch here upon the inaccessible mystery of evil with its many layers of impenetrability. "That which I had the strength to do, I lack the strength to undo.... That which I was too weak to avoid doing, I will remain unable to erase entirely.... The worst is not perhaps to be unable to change our acts; it is that our acts change us to the point that we can no longer change ourselves."[3] Our most radical helplessness is that we can in no way delete our sins against the Holy One. They can only be forgiven by God. That dependence is probably the hardest part of the living on forgiveness. Most of us are such ingrained do-it-yourselfers that it is most unpleasant for us to run into a situation where we are mere receivers. Our natural tendency is to feel better when we are in control.

There is a charming legend about St. Jerome which brings this truth home to us in a profound and clear way.[4] Most readers will know that St. Jerome in his later years lived a kind of hermit life near Bethlehem. Less well known is the fact that in his younger years he also attempted to be a recluse, this time in a desert near Chalcis in Syria. During his first attempt, young Jerome fell into a state of serious depression which showed that at this age he was not yet called to such a life. While he was at the nadir of distress, the crucified Jesus is said to have appeared to him. Jerome immediately fell on his knees, bent low, and with a broad gesture struck his breast. Jesus on his cross smiles gently and asks him: "Jerome, what do you have to offer me?" Jerome is delighted and quick to respond, "Everything, Lord, above all the loneliness of this desert which is so hard on me." The Lord thanks him graciously, and then asks again, "What more, Jerome, do you have to offer me?" Without hesitating Jerome replies, "My fasting, my hunger and my thirst;" and he even adds a little clarification, explaining that he does neither eat nor drink before sunset. Jesus on his cross expresses his deep appreciation and empathy; after all, he himself had some experience of fasting in the desert. Jesus repeats his question several times, "What else do you offer me, Jerome?" Jerome is never short of an answer, sometimes even rather talkative: his night watches, the prayer of the psalms, the reading of scripture. Each time the crucified Jesus thanks him with a smile, and continues repeating the question. Jerome manages to find new answers: "The celibacy which I try to live as best I can; the lack of comfort in this barren place; the heat of the day and the cold of the night." But eventually Jerome reaches the end of his wits and throws up his arms, utterly frustrated that the Lord is still not satisfied with such an impressive list of his heroic sacrifices. Then there was a deep stillness in the hermitage and in the whole Syrian desert as Jesus looked lovingly at Jerome and said, "There is one thing you have forgotten, Jerome. Give me also your sins, that I may forgive them."

All the things that Jerome mentioned were his own accomplishments. The one thing he could not do himself, he forgot. No wonder he was depressed. In all of his answers Jerome was always the achiever. In the forgiveness of his sins, though, the person of Jesus and the good news of his redemption would be central, and Jerome would be at the receiving end.

If Jesus were to ask us the same question, undoubtedly our list of responses would be quite different; but we would probably make the same mistake as Jerome. We, too, might forget to let ourselves be gifted with the gift that only God can give: the forgiveness of our sins. God delights in showing mercy, Micah says (7:18). Let us not deprive God of this delight.

5. Love's Completion

The reception of the gift of forgiveness is not a private affair. It has a worldwide dimension. Jesus, by his death and resurrection, reconciled all of humankind with God and opened the road to light and peace for all. "God delivered us from the power of darkness and transferred us to the kingdom of his beloved Son, in whom we have redemption, the forgiveness of sins." (Col 1:13–14). The nearest part of our world that needs reconciliation is always myself. In this way redemption progresses in our world, and the kingdom of God grows among us. To confess our sins is a deeply personal act and therefore has universal impact.

Divine forgiveness is a process that finds its clearest expression in the sacrament of reconciliation. In this process we quite naturally distinguish three phases.

First, there is the preparation in which we let our sins surface as far as this is reasonably possible. The most profitable approach is not by way of introspection, but rather by contemplating Jesus, especially in his passion. Thus we may also avoid wallowing in a poor self-image ("I am no good") and be able to accept in a healthy and mature way our own responsibility for what we did or did not do. Moreover, it is good to keep in mind that there is no way in which we can fully articulate our guilt (think of the image of the iceberg); neither God nor the church demands this from us. An important part of the preparation is that we open our hearts for the grace of contrition, preferably again by focusing on the crucified Jesus. The following prayer might be used:

Tell me, Jesus
my Master and my Lord,
nailed on the cross
between criminals,
tell me, Jesus,
which love for me
has turned you, my Creator,
into that man
without appearance or beauty,
dying for my sins,
that man crucified,
who gives his life
as an offering for me.
Tell me, Jesus,
how you can
thus
give your life
for me.

Tell me, Jesus,
my Master and my Lord,
nailed on the cross
between criminals,
tell me, Jesus
which love for you
will turn me, poor sinner
into a person with a contrite and broken heart,
weeping for my sins,
a person, who is forgiven
and wants to live for you.
Tell me, Jesus,
how I can
also
give my life
for you.[1]

After the preparation follows the central part of the process:
the actual confession of our guilt to God through his representative and the absolution of our sins, spoken in the name of God.

The last and very important part of the process is the time spent in absorbing and relishing God's forgiveness. God forgives infinitely fast, but *we* need a lot of time to assimilate this forgiveness completely and to let it enfold us in all its healing effects. We shall experience a light heart, a feeling that the shackles have dropped from us. It will not surprise us that this third part really requires time, if we consider that forgiveness is an extreme form of love. We have to let it permeate our whole being and penetrate into the darkest corners of our restlessness and repression. I fear that to a large extent we have neglected this step in our traditional practice of confession. This has robbed the sacrament of a vital part of its beauty. The process of reconciliation has only come to completion when we are reconciled with ourselves and are able to forgive ourselves. So far does the wonder of God's forgiveness extend.

The father of the prodigal son experienced a deep, enormous joy when he embraced his lost and returned son and clothed him with his love, as with a festive garment. Jesus says, "No one knows the Father except the Son and anyone to whom the Son wishes to reveal him" (Mt 11:27). In all three parables of Luke 15, Jesus reveals to us something essential of the Father, namely his tremendous joy in forgiving.

In one of his short stories Werner Bergengrün writes the profound sentence: "Love proves its genuineness in fidelity, but it reaches its completion in forgiveness."[2] When I read these words, they immediately imprinted themselves on my memory, and I have often repeated them. The image which first came to my mind was of a loving elderly couple, whose youthful lovesickness developed through the years into a mature love, which proved its authenticity in decades of faithfulness. However, when one is able to forgive the spouse of a serious wrongdoing, then love reaches its completion. It later dawned on me that these words of Bergengrün also apply to God. God's love, too, proves its genuineness in fidelity and reaches its completion in forgiveness. Since God IS love, we can say that God's essential being comes to fulfillment in forgiveness. Then, to a certain degree, we can understand why God finds such an overflowing joy in forgiving. In the well-known text of Zephaniah this exuberant joy is portrayed:

> Shout for joy, O daughter Zion! sing joyfully, O Israel!
> Be glad and exult with all your heart, O daughter Jerusalem!
> The Lord has removed the judgment against you,
> he has turned away your enemies.
> The King of Israel, the Lord, is in your midst,
> you have no further misfortune to fear.
> On that day, it shall be said to Jerusalem:
> Fear not, O Zion, be not discouraged!
> The Lord, your God, is in your midst, a mighty savior;
> He will rejoice over you with gladness,
> and renew you in his love,
> He will sing joyfully because of you, as one sings at festivals
> (3:14–17).

In the parable of the refound father, this joy seems to be expressed even more profoundly. The crowning moment of divine forgiveness is when this joy of the Father flows over into us and fills our hearts. The vocabulary of the father includes the words joy, celebration, feast, new life, to be found. The terminology of the son is: hunger, misery, pods, pigs, unworthiness, hired worker. The son is transported into the world of his father, from darkness and gloom into light and peace.

> Someone
> must come to us from the future
> prodigally
> with rings and robes and kisses
> and fall upon our self-reproach
> with the tears of welcome.
> (John Shea)

During the 1983 Synod of Bishops, whose theme was penance and reconciliation, a group of African bishops emphasized the importance of joy in the celebration of reconciliation. The penance service and the sacrament of reconciliation should not be endured, but celebrated. Already St. Augustine, in his famous *Confessions*, transformed the confession of his sins into a *confessio laudis* (a hymn of praise).

A New Intimacy

In sharing God's joy, we draw closer to God, just as the prodigal son did when he was engulfed in his father's happiness. Before the younger son returned home, both brothers knew that their father was a good man; however, *how* good he was only the younger one discovered, and he did so precisely in his being forgiven. At that moment an intimacy grew between father and son, which had tremendous depth and endured for a lifetime. In the joy of the father it dawned on the son how much this man had loved him and still loved him.

The Canticle of Zechariah expresses very appropriately, that by the forgiveness of their sins, God will give the people (experiential) knowledge of salvation. It is an awesome aspect of the good news that the experience of new life takes place precisely when we are most at a loss, and that God's mercy touches us most deeply where our sinfulness makes us most vulnerable. Prior to the experience of reconciliation our image of God was vague and we had only a very remote concept of divine love. Then *in* the forgiveness, God's mercy becomes so much more real to us. Our infidelity does not exhaust God's love but reveals its unconditional and limitless dimensions. As we come before God with the broken pieces of our lives, we are not rejected or condemned, but welcomed with great tenderness.

It is so easy to say that God's love is based on nothing, is fathomless; in the forgiveness we may experience this (as far as humanly possible). Jesus in the gospel never belittles sin; he forgives it. His mercy is large enough to deal with it in all its evil. He can afford to take it seriously. For us, it takes courage, honesty and patience to digest this awesome reality in its two vast dimensions.

God takes our sin extremely seriously. It is the complete opposite of God's being, which is love. It is one of the most breathtaking mysteries of creation, that we are free to reject the divine love to which we owe our very existence. It is like being able to saw off the branch on which we sit and still survive. To consider this mystery in depth can make one dizzy. Correspondingly, God does not simply dismiss sin with a light gesture. The Holy One confronts it in all its ruthless and lethal reality, precisely because the Most High takes us humans—also in our sin—very seriously. The God of the covenant and of faithfulness answers for the guilt of those who were not faithful. This becomes for the loving God in the Son's passion love's ordeal: "For our sake God made him to be sin who did not know sin, so that we might become the righteousness of God in him" (2 Cor 5,21).

Forgiveness is awesome. The price of the reconciliation was infinitely high. God paid it. In the forgiveness both the mercy and the omnipotence of God are revealed. A classical prayer in the Roman missal articulates: "Abba, in your unbounded mercy, you have revealed the beauty of your power through your constant forgiveness of our sins. Continue to fill us with your gifts of love."[3]

A rabbi used the simple image of a cord. Each person is connected to God by a cord. When we sin, the cord is severed. In reconciliation God ties the two loose ends together in a knot. The bond is restored and...the cord has become shorter. We have come closer to God in the process. With the prophet Micah we can proclaim in wonder, "Who is there like you, the God who removes guilt and pardons sin for the remnant of your inheritance; who does not persist in anger forever, but delights rather in clemency" (7:18).

A retreatant once told me a dream which captures beautifully the key message of this chapter. I am pleased that she allows me to share it with you.

"I found myself in the school playground of my childhood. There were several baskets filled with dark brown pieces of broken pottery which I had to spread out on the ground while a large crowd watched me. They knew very well that those shards were the broken pieces of my life—all that I had messed up. As I squatted, I took the pieces out of the baskets. They were of every size and shape: small and large, flat and curved. Many of them had sharp edges on which I occasionally cut my hand. Deeply ashamed, blushing intensely, depressed and humiliated in the sight of all those people, I kept exposing all the potsherds.

"Suddenly a change took place. The ugly brown shards turned into colorful glass fragments: red and blue, yellow and green, orange and purple: a full array of colors. The sunlight shone through them. I stood up to have a better view.

"I was overcome with surprise. All these pieces formed an exquisite mosaic of extraordinary and unforeseen beauty. I stood and watched in wonder and sheer delight."

> I love you
> because you are helping me to make
> of the lumber of my life
> not a tavern
> but a temple;
> out of the works of my every day
> not a reproach
> but a song.
>
> (Roy Croft)

III

MISSION

6. Our Life as a Mission

We long for our experience of reconciliation to be celebrated and shared. One cannot keep for oneself the joy which the new discovery of God's goodness has touched off. Forgiveness transforms a person into an apostle. Reconciliation leads to mission. "Give me again the joy of your help; with a spirit of fervor sustain me, that I may teach transgressors your ways and sinners may return to you" (Ps 51:14–15; cf. 16–17).

In our day the word "mission" usually means a task to be accomplished, oftentimes with the connotation of something difficult or challenging, and possibly of a going forth. In the Bible the emphasis is different. Neither the difficulty nor the distance are essential, but rather the close personal union between the person sending and the person sent. The late Father James Walsh, S.J., used to say, "The heart of the mission is the indwelling!" That was a truly biblical approach.

In scripture, mission is first of all making the other person present, a "substituting" for the other person. Mission means to refer to the one who sent. The person sent speaks and acts in the name and with the authority of the person sending. In Hebrew the person missioned is called *shaliach*, and a well-known principle states, "The one sent by a person is like that person himself." Whether this mission requires a going forth or not is secondary. What constitutes the mission is the personal union and the transparency, so that the person sending becomes present in the one sent. Obviously, this requires a great deal of selflessness in the person who accepts a mission in this biblical sense of the word.

In the Old Testament we find many examples which illustrate the concept of mission. Normally the dividing line between God and God's messenger is very thin. Often in the beginning of a story the angel of Yahweh appears, who then later on in the narrative is simply called God. So the angel is completely identified with God, is a manifestation of God in angelic form.[1]

In the New Testament Jesus summarizes the gist of mission in the twofold verse, "Amen, amen, I say to you, whoever receives the one I send receives me, and whoever receives me receives the one who sent me" (Jn 13,20). He repeats the same principle but with more stress on the negative aspect: "Whoever listens to you listens to me. Whoever rejects you rejects me. And whoever rejects me rejects the one who sent me (Lk 10,16). In this perspective the missioning in Mark's gospel is clearer: "He appointed twelve (whom he also named apostles) that they might be with him and he might send them forth to preach" (3:14), where the being with him and the being sent forth are two aspects of mission and not two separate parts.

Everyone Has a Mission

If we interpret mission the way scripture does, we understand that in the church every Christian is sent. Once again this does not mean that each Christian has to travel to another place, let alone to foreign countries, but that we are all called to labor in communion with Christ. This implies a liberation from egocentrism and an opening up to Jesus. This kind of mission is essential for the church and for each person in the church. It is in this way that faith grows, and in the first place, our own faith. A church which is preoccupied too much with itself loses its vibrancy and credibility. The final document of the extraordinary Synod of Bishops held in 1985 states: "Christ is the light of humanity. The church, proclaiming the Gospel, must see to it that this light clearly shines out from her countenance. The church makes herself more credible if she speaks less of herself and ever more preaches Christ crucified (cf. 1 Cor 2:2) and witnesses with her own life."[2] Similarly, in the individual Christian, faith, hope and love come to full bloom only when they are shared. That is the secret of the rapid growth of the early church. Today the same opportunities and challenges are there. Pope John Paul II brought this home forcefully in his encyclical *Redemptoris Missio* (1991), which he himself captured in these words: "Missionary activity renews the church, revitalizes faith and Christian identity, and offers fresh enthusiasm and new incentives. Faith is strengthened when it is shared with others."

The Second Vatican Council provided new momentum to this missionary outreach. The implementation of its vision has literally transformed the face of our parishes. Unlike the past, today it would be impossible for a parish to function without the numerous services of full and part-time lay co-workers, many of whom are volunteers. In its Decree on the Laity, the council makes this significant statement: "In the church, there is diversity in ministry, but unity in mission."[3] It is in mission that all Christians are united. Mission is basic; it ties in directly with baptism. Compared to mission, the distinction between clerics and lay people is secondary.

The psalms tell us to praise God on the ten-stringed lute (33:2, 92:4, 144:9). It reminds me of the story of a retired engineer who happened to inherit a cello. Alas, all the strings except one were broken. Nevertheless, each day undauntedly he played his instrument for several hours. One day in exasperation his wife lost her patience and protested that other cellos she had seen always had four strings. "Moreover," she added, "those cellists keep moving the fingers of their left hand all the time. You don't do that either." "You have to understand," he replied, "They are looking for the right place: I have found it." While it is obvious that neither human beings, nor God could be pleased with that type of music, yet mission is an instrument with far more than four or ten strings. There is a tremendous variety of ministries and charisms in the church. It is the sense of mission which establishes the harmony in this diversity.

Because mission is primary, it can overcome old and new forms of clericalism, bridge many differences, and ease unhealthy tensions in our communities. In the literal sense of

the word, mission relativizes: i.e., establishes a relationship to
the one who sends, namely the risen Jesus, and in doing so
makes the mission relative. In mission the emphasis is not so
much on us, but rather on God who, in Jesus, missions. In this
way mission creates unity without discarding pluriformity. Jesus
sends not only a particular person, he sends all the others as
well. When the one who missions all becomes more distinctly
the center, then working together becomes more harmonious
and witnessing more credible. Because the fathers of Vatican II
foresaw possible difficulties, they asserted in one of the most
important documents, the Constitution on the Church *Lumen
Gentium*:

> Pastors know that they themselves were not meant by Christ to
> shoulder alone the entire saving mission of the church toward the
> world. On the contrary, they understand that it is their noble
> duty so to shepherd the faithful and recognize their services and
> charismatic gifts that all according to their proper roles may
> cooperate in this common undertaking with one heart (LG 30).

They also promulgated:

> Let sacred pastors recognize and promote the dignity as well as
> the responsibility of lay people in the church. Let them willingly
> make use of their prudent advice. Let them confidently assign
> duties to them in the service of the church, allowing them free-
> dom and room for action. Further, let them encourage the lay
> people so that they may undertake tasks on their own initiative.
> Attentively in Christ, let them consider with fatherly love the pro-
> jects, suggestions, and desires proposed by the laity.
> Furthermore, let pastors respectfully acknowledge that just free-
> dom which belongs to everyone in this earthly city (LG 37).

It is imperative that all Christians discover and discern their
own vocation ever more clearly so that the community becomes
more convincingly the place where God's love is made tangible,
and where the Christian faith is conveyed in our secularized
world.

God chose us to show
   the face of God's love
to one another.
We are God's vocabulary;
   living words
to give voice to God's goodness
   in and through our goodness,
To give voice to God's compassion,
   tenderness, caring, faithfulness
in and through us.

                     (Leo Rock, S.J.)

In this discernment of the personal mission, we definitely need each other. A basic conviction such as Cardinal Newman voiced is, of course, very helpful, if not indispensable:

God has created me to do Him some definite service; He has committed some work to me which he has not committed to another. I have my mission—I never may know it in this life, but I shall be told it in the next. Somehow I am necessary for His purposes, as necessary in my place as an Archangel in his—if, indeed, I fail, He can raise another, as He could make the stones children of Abraham. Yet I have a part in this great work; I am a link in a chain, a bond of connection between persons. He has not created me for naught. I shall do good, I shall do His work; I shall be an angel of peace, a preacher of truth in my own place, while not intending it, if I do but keep His commandments and serve Him in my calling.[4]

7. As the Father Has Sent Me

✦

The Paschal Mission

In each of the four gospels there are several instances during the public life of Jesus, in which he sends his disciples on a mission (e.g., in Luke's gospel: 5:1–11; 6:12–16; 9:1–6; 10:1–16). No matter how significant these missions are, they seem to be only preludes to the final mission by the risen Lord after his resurrection. All appearances of the risen Jesus culminate in a missioning which knows no boundaries. The finale of Matthew's gospel highlights the all-encompassing scope of this mission in a four-fold universality:

- Universal power in heaven and on earth is given to the one who conquered death and the origin of death, sin. By overcoming these two most formidable powers he has obtained dominion over all others as well.
- All nations in space and time are included in this mission, which is indeed global and continual. The good news has to be brought to every person on earth.
- All that Jesus commanded his disciples must be handed on. The message is not to be reduced by tailoring it to suit particular tastes. It is to be preached in its catholicity; i.e., in its universality and entirety.
- Always, until the end of time, Jesus will be with those he

48

sends. The mission hinges on this real though invisible nearness of the risen Lord. He is present and active in his disciples. In the first chapter of Matthew the child to be born was announced as Emmanuel, "God is with us" (v 23). In the last line of the same gospel the full extent of this promise is revealed.

Only the Son who, in the power of the Holy Spirit, is resurrected from the dead by the Almighty, can send in such plenitude. In him the reign of God has come in its fullness. The resurrection of Jesus implies for each of us that the risen Christ has taken charge of our lives and transformed them into a mission.

The content of mission is always in one form or another to announce the risen Jesus and to spread the seed of the resurrection. In Acts 1:22, Peter gives a definition of an apostle in the words: "To be with us (i.e., in communion with the other disciples) a witness to Christ's resurrection." This implies that the mission shares in the joy of Easter.

A significant characteristic of this mission is that each day we receive it anew. We cannot accept our mission once and for all, because that would be to annex it and then it would no longer be a mission. A mission taken over is a self-contradiction. Since the heart of it is the relationship between the sender and the sent, a mission cannot be possessed: on the contrary, it requires a daily abandonment to the one who missions. Mission means precisely that we are no longer in control of our own life—someone else is.

There are several beautiful prayers of abandonment. One of them is that of the extraordinary farmer-councilor, father of a family of 10, Saint Nicholas von Flue (†1487), patron of Switzerland:

> My Lord and my God
> take everything from me
> that hinders my coming toward you.
>
> My Lord and my God
> give me everything
> that leads me to you.
>
> My Lord and my God

take me from myself
and give me completely
to you as your own.

Another such prayer is the concluding prayer of the Spiritual Exercises of St. Ignatius:

Take, Lord, and receive all my liberty,
my memory, my understanding, and my entire will,
all that I have and call my own.
You have given it all to me.
To you, Lord, I return it.
Everything is yours; do with it what you will.
Give me only your love and your grace.
That is enough for me (234).

Well known, also, is the prayer of Charles de Foucauld: (†1916)

Father,

I abandon myself into your hands;
do with me what you will.
Whatever you may do, I thank you:
I am ready for all, I accept all.
Let only your will be done in me,
and in all your creatures—
I wish no more than this, O Lord.
Into your hands I commend my soul;
I offer it to you with all the love, of my heart,
for I love you Lord,
and so need to give myself,
to surrender myself into your hand

without reserve,
and with boundless confidence,

for you are my father.

The oldest and shortest of them all is Mary's fiat (Lk 1:38).
    These and similar prayers of abandonment[1] can never be rec-

ommended enough; yet they are mere words. Mission, however, is abandonment, not just in words, but in the reality of daily life. This is ever a challenge, for mission presupposes the willingness to follow the call of others in their unpredictable decisions. This keeps our life in suspension. Those who are sent are fully present with heart and soul and body, and at the same time they are free to be missioned to another task or to another place. This requires great resilience. Sometimes a person sent backslides to either a certain restlessness (not being "there" wholeheartedly), or to immovability; in both cases the healthy tension of the mission is given up. The word mission is meaningful and makes sense only as long as one is open to the directions of another who, therefore, thinks and judges differently.

It is not easy to keep the sense of mission alive. Think of a religious who after many years receives a new assignment; this may well bring with it pain and setbacks, which, however, can deepen and purify the commitment. Or think of parents in whose family considerable change takes place. It is pivotal that the sense of mission does not diminish but rather grows through the years. Mission, after all, is the concrete shape of our surrender to and love of the Lord.

In one of his retreats Cardinal Carlo Martini, S.J., of Milan[2] describes four causes that can diminish the sense of mission:

- Lack of prayer, either in the time given to it or in its quality;
- Stalled spiritual growth and insufficient integration of the spiritual, intellectual and affective dimensions;
- Lack of discipline in the physical realm: food and drink, exercise, sleep, etc.
- Lack of basic integrity (literally that our life has become a cunning lie).

The Mission of Jesus

On two occasions Jesus speaks an almost identical sentence, "As the Father has sent me, so I send you." The first time was in his high-priestly prayer shortly before his passion (Jn 17:18).; the second time was on the day of his resurrection (Jn 20:21). Jesus is, in fact, saying to us that our mission is a continuation of his. So, to fully understand our mission, we have to reflect carefully on the mission of Jesus so as to conform our thinking, our priorities, and our actions to him. John's gospel especially is replete with passages that witness to the vital importance of mission in the life of Jesus. It would not be an exaggeration to say that Jesus' life is completely shaped by his mission. He never did "his own thing," but always sought the will of his Abba:

- My food is to do the will of the one who sent me and to finish his work (Jn 4:34).
- I came down from heaven not to do my own will but the will of the one who sent me (6:38).
- I know the Father, because I am from him, and he sent me (7:29).
- The one who sent me is with me. He has not left me alone, because I always do what is pleasing to him (8:29).

It is fascinating to notice how Jesus' sense of mission formed the basis for his extraordinary relational skills. In his dealings with people, he was never fearful of anyone nor was he restrained by any taboo; he was a perfectly free person. He put this exceptional freedom completely at the service of others. He gave every person he met his undivided attention without even a trace of self-concern. The people he met experienced this encounter as amazingly wholesome and freeing. He called forth the very best in each person. In the presence of Jesus people could fully be themselves. With Jesus there was room for everyone. He never had the slightest temptation to exploit or manipulate, let alone to write off anyone. In no way did he shy away from meeting people, yet in all his contacts he was never shallow or self-centered. Neither did he fear confrontation or conflict, nor on these occasions would he ever lose his composure or his peace of heart. Always there was a genuine, warm concern for the true self of the other person without ever boxing someone in. With a wonderful ease he related to people in sincere and heartfelt affection.

This striking gift of communicating is intriguing. Yet, its secret is given away on every page of the gospel. The center of Jesus' own personality and of his behavior was his Abba. His Abba was his life. At any moment he would speak about him with warm spontaneity. His intimacy with his Abba and their unreserved love for one another was obvious. His Abba relationship was clearly undisturbed, unobscured and without the slightest hint of any complex. This union with his Abba was the all-encompassing and all-determining strength of his personality, the alpha and omega of his life. From the serenity and security of this closeness, Jesus drew his vitality and his openness. His mission, in fact, was nothing but the singular living out of this Abba relationship in his daily life.

Consequently Jesus' mission had deep roots. Its origin reaches back into the bosom of the blessed Trinity, the source of all love and life. In classical theology the *processio* (i.e., the begetting of the Son through the Father in the Holy Spirit) is identical with the *missio* (i.e., the divine missioning of the only begotten to humankind). "When the fullness of time had come" (Gal 4:4), the *processio* evolved into the *missio*, the Word became flesh, sent into the world to share and redeem human life. This is to say that in Jesus, person and mission are one and the same. He identifies completely with his mission. He has no reservations, holds nothing back. His mission is void of fissures.

The manner in which Jesus lived his mission is unique. Precisely in his mission he is God's Son incarnate. In Jesus the presence of the one who sends in the person sent is unsurpassable: "The Father and I are one" (Jn 10:30). That made his demeanor so harmonious and salvific. One senses the oneness between Jesus and his Abba, and therefore also between Jesus and himself. Obedience to his mission led to his death, even his death on a cross, but then also to a name that is above every name (cf. Phil 2:8–9), and that manifests his divine identity.

Jesus lived only thirty-three years. Though this age matches more or less the median life expectancy of his time, we consider it as short—too short, really. His life was spent in a small country on the Mediterranean, which he never left. It would have been a shame if his mission remained restricted to such a small space and period of time. That is where we come into the picture. The

Almighty needs us to continue the mission of the Son, and the Holy Spirit seeks tirelessly for another body in which to prolong the incarnation. In the fullest sense of the word Jesus can say: "I have no hands but yours." Accordingly, the farewell message of the risen One is, "As the Father has sent me, so I send you" (Jn 20:21).

The mission of every Christian is clearly outlined for us in Paul's letter to the Romans: "Those God foreknew God also predestined to be conformed to the image (in Greek, *icon*) of the Son, so that he might be the first born among many brothers and sisters" (8:29). For Theilhard de Chardin this text in its context (v 18–39) is the great hymn of hope just as 1 Corinthians 13 is the great hymn of love. He paraphrases: "There is only one event in the whole of history: the Incarnation." The entire process of cosmic evolution reaches its peak and completion in point Omega, when Christ has integrated all into his person. The conviction that Christ lives on in all Christians is expressed clearly by both Paul and John. Paul states, "I live, not with my own life, but with the life of Christ who lives in me" (Gal 2:20, *JB*). John presents the rich image of the branches, which can only bear fruit as long as the sap of the vine circulates through them (Jn 15). Negatively it is said: "Just as a branch cannot bear fruit on its own unless it remains on the vine, so neither can you unless you remain in me." And positively we are told: "Whoever remains in me and I in him will bear much fruit." Hence, without our union with the Lord there is no fruit at all, whereas united with him, we bear much fruit. That is reassuring. An even greater fruitfulness can be obtained, when the branch is pruned (v 2).

Trinitarian Mission

Two verses in John's gospel are identical except for one word. John 20:21 reads: "As the Father has sent me, so I send you." In John 15:9 we find: "As the Father has loved me, so I love you." Evidently the words love and mission are interchangeable. Mission is the concrete shape of love in many ways. The love of the Holy One to the Son is the origin of all mission, while the love of the Son to his Abba is its driving force. The love of the triune God for us concretizes itself in the mission, just as our love for God and for each other takes shape in mission. Mission is always a percolation of God's love reaching our neighbor through the person sent.

In the beginning of time God's love created the universe, thus manifesting itself. It can be found and experienced, therefore, in all things. In the fullness of time God's love became incarnate in the Word made flesh in the person of Jesus. "We saw his glory...and from his fullness we have all received grace upon grace" (Jn 1:14–18). In the present time this love continues through the people who open themselves up for the mission, so that it can reach in a tangible and human way the men and women of today. Thus, the content of the mission is indeed the ever more unfolding love that God has for us and to which we try to respond. Although the purpose of our life is a return to God from whom we came, we cannot bypass the world in our returning home. It is not our return to God which is primary, but our sharing in God's reaching out into the world.

In Ignatian spirituality the apostolic mission takes the prime place. In 1538, even before they had decided to form into a religious order, the "friends in the Lord" offered their little company to the pope in fulfillment of their vows made at Montmartre, Paris, August 15, 1534. They expressed their readiness to be sent wherever the greater glory of God and service to the people would be hoped for. This commitment was interpreted unambiguously in a trinitarian perspective as recorded in the Spiritual Diary of St. Ignatius: "I felt a desire to consider other insights which came to me, namely, how the Son first sent the apostles to preach in poverty; and then how the Holy Spirit, by communicating himself and the gift of tongues, confirmed them; and how, thus, when the Father and the Son sent the Holy Spirit, all three Persons confirmed that mission."[3] A modern commentary explains: "Apostolic mission shares in the trinitarian salvific love of God, which turns itself toward the world. Ignatius uses the same word for the "sending" of the apostles to preach in poverty as for the "sending" of the Holy Spirit by the Father and Son, namely *inviare*. This suggests how deeply in the vision of Ignatius the apostle is taken up into the very life of the blessed Trinity."[4]

8. How Jesus Sends

The trinitarian origin of the mission is not just a dogmatic doctrine, but it also provides us with very practical ways of how to make our mission fruitful. Jesus says, "It was not you who chose me, but I who chose you and appointed you to go and bear fruit that will remain" (Jn 15:16). A little earlier he had said, "By this is my Father glorified, that you bear much fruit and become my disciples" (Jn 15:8). Immediately following, he reveals to us the secret of that fruitfulness: "As the Father loves me, so I also love you. Remain in my love" (Jn 15:9). According to Jesus' words, it is not enough to think from time to time of this love or to pay an occasional visit there; we have to make it our home, just as Jesus had his home with his Abba. The one purpose of his life was to lead us into intimacy with his Father and the Holy Spirit, in whom he was always rooted himself. This will free us from fear, saying with Jesus in the Holy Spirit: "Abba" (cf. Rom 8:14–15).

Not Self-Sufficient

When Jesus sent the seventy-two disciples, he said to them: "The harvest is abundant but the laborers are few." One would expect that he would follow that statement with an appeal to *work* all the harder. Instead he enjoins us to *pray*: "So ask the master of the harvest to send out laborers for his harvest" (Lk 10:2). Ask! We may ask that God send others; in the Christian tradition the prayer for vocations has always had a valuable place. Also, we may ask that God send us. One thing is sure: we can only work in the vineyard when we are missioned. In the parable of the workers in the vineyard, the landowner asks the people who still stand in the marketplace at 5 p.m.: "Why do you stand here idle all day?" Their answer was to the point: "Because no one has hired us" (Mt 20:6).

In his letter to the Romans, Paul asks the rhetorical question: "How can people preach unless they are sent?" (10:15). One might add: "*What* are they to preach if they are not sent?" Or, still more pertinent: "*Whom* are they to preach?" Themselves?

Mission is always a call beyond professionalism. This is to say, that professional expertise is definitely required, but is also insufficient. This accounts for the common, painful experience that no training for ministry will ever be adequate. It also guards us from straining or forcing. What is at stake is not something we could reach with a little more effort. It is a dimension to which we simply have no access on our own.

Our mission must be rooted in the "Beyond," and becomes fruitful in the degree that the "Beyond" comes through. Once again, this is the wisdom of the biblical concept of mission.

Jesus is the perfect example. Wherever he got his education, he was clearly superbly qualified for his ministry. Yet, his real strength was not his professionalism, but the fact that the "Beyond" shone through in an unsurpassable degree. His oneness with the Father was his ultimate secret.

The mission must be accepted, but cannot be demanded. It is the sender's prerogative to mission someone: "It was not you who chose me, but I who chose you and appointed you..." (Jn 15:16). In Mark's gospel we are similarly reminded, "Jesus went up the mountain and summoned those whom he wanted" (Mk 3:13). Mission is Jesus' initiative and requires from us that we fit ourselves into the work of salvation which he accomplishes through us. He does not necessarily send us where we experience the greatest satisfaction, show to the best advantage, or unfold our talents best. He also applies other criteria, which may well come first. The mission which he entrusts to us, may be quite provocative and unattractive. Of one thing we can be assured: it will bring peace and freedom to many, ourselves included.

There is a subtle but important distinction between working for God and doing God's work, as Thomas H. Green, S.J., has pointed out.[1] The first phrase reminds me of a free-lance professional who refuses long-term commitments, decides independently which work to take on, and then offers the end product to the highest bidder. In this particular case, the end product would be proffered to God, but it remains to be seen whether God accepts it or not. In the other case, the decision, what to do, is with the Holy One, who can freely dispose of the person sent. It is God's work from the very beginning.

The entire thrust of the thirty-day Spiritual Exercises of St. Ignatius is to distinguish what God wants us to do from what we ourselves want to do for God. It is not enough that we serve the Almighty according to our own liking and, in fact, do our own thing; no, God must be able to dispose of us entirely and freely. We can be sure that God's will is never a threat to our true well-being. God loves us more than we love ourselves!

God is our ultimate concern, for we owe the Most High our very being. People usually want some*thing* from us: our money, our time, our skills, our contacts, etc. God wants *us*, in the fullest sense of the word. That is what we call creation. The Almighty takes us one hundred percent seriously and concretizes this in entrusting a mission to us. This certainly implies a burden, and requires of us discipline, dedication, selflessness, and above all, trust. There is so little that we can substantiate, let alone prove or control. There is only our confidence in God on whom we build entirely. It is sheer faith.

On the other hand, the acceptance of this arrangement also brings with it a tremendous relief. Our task is transferred from a merely ethical level to the realm of personal relationship in which the one who sends is present and active in the person sent. The letter to the Hebrews concludes with the prayerful wish that the God of peace "may carry out in us what is pleasing to him" (13:21). In this way we are freed from the pressure of having to achieve all by ourselves. It would be a "divinity complex"[2] if we would act as if the salvation of the world rests solely on our shoulders. Once we understand what scripture means by mission, then we are totally liberated from such self-imposed burdens. In the Bible God "has accomplished all we have done" (Is 26:12) and "we are his handiwork created in Christ Jesus for the good works that God has prepared in advance" (Eph 2:10). Ours is only the mop-up operation.

Cooperation could be understood as if our activity would be an addition to God's work, or vice versa. This is obviously a misunderstanding. God does everything, and so do we: God in the divine way and we in the human way. Sometimes it is called *synergy*. The word of itself is not important. Significant is the insight, how our activity is completely permeated and supported by God's action. This awareness gives us peace and tranquility, saves us from discouragement and bigotry, and releases in us a gentle strength.

Trusting in the Lord

When Jesus missioned the seventy-two disciples, he challenged them: "Carry no money bag, no sack, no sandals" (Lk 10:4). Take only peace as your luggage. It sounds very rigorous. Yet, let us first hear in these words the concern that he has for us. We worry about running short or lacking something, and so our immediate impulse is to hoard or to procure a respectable credit card. Jesus' worry, on the contrary, is that we might have too much, and that as a consequence, our vitality and fruitfulness become stifled. "As for the seed that fell among thorns, they are the ones who have heard the word of God, but as they go along, they are choked by the anxieties and riches and pleasures of life, and they fail to produce mature fruit" (Lk 8:14). Oftentimes in our anxiety we seek to bolster ourselves by accumulating all kinds of assets, yet deep in our hearts we know very well that our insecurity cannot be overcome by material things. Jesus wants to spare us this trap.

What we might perceive as an exaggerated demand, is in the first place an encouragement to place our trust in God. This touches the heart of every mission. A mission without trust in the sender is nothing but a caricature. The heart of poverty is our letting go of self and entrusting ourselves to God. That is why poverty and mission are so closely connected that only a mission in poverty is wholly credible. A Hindu professor in India, writing to a priest friend, acknowledged many of the values of the Catholic Church, but also shared two critical observations. The first is that we talk too much in committees, meetings, task forces, liturgies and the like. The second one was that we are too well equipped and endowed. Both insights seem to be related and to point to the fact that we have a tendency to be in control. It seems that these two flaws hindered this distinguished person from finding God in our church.

In the western world we are quick to assert the opposite position by pointing out that in our culture if one is to be relevant in one's mission, a respectable standard of living is needed. Although there is some truth in that statement, Jesus never bothered to teach it. He always preached and lived poverty. It is in this area that we readily find reasons to water down the gospel message. It is not uncommon to grant ourselves great leeway in interpreting Jesus' instructions about being poor. Today's affluent society, with its conspicuous overconsumption propels us ever more subtly and relentlessly in the wrong direction. A missionary once remarked at the end of his home leave, with a twinkle in his eye, "I am happy to go back from the poverty of wealth to the wealth of poverty." If we are truly seeking to walk in the footsteps of Jesus, it is essential that we deliberately and resolutely keep in step with the poor Jesus. Otherwise, there is no way in this consumer society that we can withstand the exterior and interior pressures toward ever greater material comfort. The result? Impairment and erosion of our mission.

From the very beginning the mission of Jesus was one of emptying himself (cf. Phil 2:7–8). We are called "to have that same attitude that also Christ Jesus had" (v 5) and to live the self-emptying of Jesus, so there is no place for striking a bargain in our mission. Certainly, "the laborer deserves his keep," yet in the same breath we are told: "Without cost you have received; without cost you are to give" (Mt 10:8,10). The clear message is that we are not to strive after our own profit whether that might mean money, career, standard of living, prestige, affirmation, recognition, influence, control, power. God will give us generously what we need for a psychologically sound and happy life, mostly through people. We are not to worry about that.

Just as Jesus found such a security in his Abba that he was freer than the foxes with their dens and the birds with their nests (cf. Lk 9:58), so we can find in Jesus so much assurance and fulfillment that we can serve without seeking gain. In Jesus we have found the fine pearl for which we gladly give up everything (cf. Mt 13:44–46). Evangelical poverty is the expression of a fulfillment and inner freedom, which enables us to live very simply. Its essence is not deficiency but fullness, not giving up much, but having found much. "In his body lives the fullness of divinity, and in him you too find your own fulfillment" (Col 2:9). A Hindu story vividly describes this inner wealth and fulfillment. May we indeed find this in Jesus.

> The sannyasi had reached the outskirts of the village and settled down under a tree for the night when a villager came running up to him and said, "The stone! The stone! Give me the precious stone!"
>
> "What stone?" asked the sannyasi.
>
> "Last night the Lord Shiva appeared to me in a dream," said the villager, "and told me that if I went to the outskirts of the village at dusk I should find a sannyasi who would give me a precious stone that would make me rich forever."
>
> The sannyasi rummaged in his bag and pulled out a stone. "He probably meant this one," he said, as he handed the stone over to the villager. "I found it on a forest path some days ago. You can certainly have it."
>
> The man looked at the stone in wonder. It was a diamond. Probably the largest diamond in the whole world for it was as large as a man's head.

He took the diamond and walked away. All night he tossed about in bed, unable to sleep. Next day at the crack of dawn he woke the sannyasi and said, "Give me the wealth that makes it possible for you to give away this diamond so easily."[3]

Jesus himself brings home to us what the forsaking of power means to us in the image of sending us "like lambs among wolves" (Lk 10:3). This applies both to the individual and the community. The history of the church gives evidence that faith was most fruitful in those periods in which the mission of the church was either barely tolerated or rejected as not in sufficient conformity to the state. Whenever the sheep or the shepherd complied too much, they achieved less good.

Of course, it is anything but an idyll to be a lamb among the wolves. The early church learned that the hard way. Nor did Jesus ever promise us an idyll. What he promised was fruitfulness and peace that the world cannot give. Precisely because the biblical mission rests in an intimate personal relationship, it is vulnerable. That which constitutes its strength, when neglected, will cause its ruin. Its heart will always be, "Remain in my love" (Jn 15:9).

IV

FRUITFULNESS

9. Missioned to Bear Fruit

A Contemplation on the Parable of the Sower

In an elaborate parable of the Sower, Jesus uses this image for the word of God: "The seed is the word of God" (Lk 8:11). The essence of the seed is to bear fruit. Similarly, the word of God, by its very nature, is meant to bring forth fruit. The amount of fruit it will produce depends mainly, as Jesus explains, on our openness to assimilate the word. A reflection on the life in the light of this teaching, if absorbed and savored leisurely, can help us bring together many facets of our life.[1] Let us dwell on the meaning of each seed in a personal way.

I find a quiet space and place myself in a reverent and relaxed position. I sense how I am present. I note attentively the various sounds and let them be. After having observed the place and settled in it, I close my eyes or focus them gently on a quiet spot. I smell the odors; they are all right. I feel my body: my clothes, the floor, the chair or the kneeler or the prayer stool, I pay attention to my breathing. I accept it all peacefully. Now I am really "there," and also apart.

Then I lift my mind to God relishing the knowledge that the Almighty watches me with love and delight. It is good to be in the gracious and attentive presence of the Holy One. I let myself be loved by God to whom I owe my whole being. The Most High supports me with a mighty hand. Though incomprehensible, it is reassuring to believe that God loves me far more than I love myself. I express my deep respect and show my gratitude.

I ask for the special grace I am seeking in this meditation; e.g., that my life may bear fruit a hundredfold, fruit that will last; or, that I may remain in God's love and live in union with the Holy One; or, that I may be able to accept myself and my own life history and in doing so may be reconciled and in peace; or, whatever petition my heart suggests.

Now I imagine myself in the midst of the crowd listening to Jesus who is teaching in a boat not far from the shore. The sun is shining; the wind blows through my hair. The light is bright. The people listen with rapt attention. Together with them I am fascinated by Jesus. After he finishes his parable, Jesus comes ashore and goes to all of his listeners giving to each of us a few seeds. As he comes to me, he looks intently at me with undivided love, radiating a great trust in me. I stretch out my hand like I do when receiving holy communion and he puts five grains of seed in the palm of my hand. I feel a strong urge now to be by myself, so I go apart from the crowd to a quiet place. The memory of his gaze still fills my heart with wonder. The way he looked at me was unique. I savor the warmth and depth, the strength and goodness, which came across so powerfully, and let them penetrate my whole being.

After awhile I take one seed and throw it on the road. In no time, a bird flies by and picks it up. Gone! I notice my feelings. I ask myself what in my life was snatched away before it had any chance to take root. What in my life has always been lacking? What have I been deprived of from the very beginning? What opportunities have I not had? How does this affect me? How do I cope with it?

When I feel satisfied, I pick up another seed. This time I toss it on rocky ground where the soil is barren. I notice how quickly it shoots up. However, when the sun shines, my seed soon withers and dies. Again, I listen to my feelings. I consider what in my life shriveled up all too soon. What turned out to be only superficial, with insufficient roots? Perhaps something at first looked very promising, yet it never developed into anything worthwhile. How do I feel about these things now? How have I lived with these disappointments?

After I have contented myself, I take a third grain and throw it among thorns. I watch as my seed shoots up, but the weeds grow faster, depriving it of light and air and soon choking it. How do I feel as I watch this happening? What in my life never reached maturity, because it "was choked by the anxieties and riches and pleasures of life" (Lk 8:14)? What never quite lived up to the expectations? What do those choking thorns look like in my life? How do I deal with them?

When the time has come, I throw the fourth grain into rich soil. I watch as it grows tall and strong and yields abundant fruit. What feelings do I experience? I look at everything in my life that has gone well and has been really fruitful. Once more I take my time to savor it all. I don't want to miss anything. I thank God "who causes the growth" (1 Cor 3:7) and gladly recognize him as the source of all good.

I still have one grain left. I feel it, rub it gently between my fingers, sense its precariousness. I marvel at its capacity to bear such wonderful fruit. This last seed carries the future in itself. It stands for the time of my life that is yet to come. I have no knowledge of how long that will be nor what it will look like. I ponder what I will do with this unknown rest of my life, insofar as it depends on me. I have learned precious lessons from my experiences with the four previous seeds. I am careful in my deliberations and don't want to hurry now. Once I have reached sufficient clarity, I consult once more with Jesus. I offer him my resolve and ask for his blessing. Then, under Jesus' gaze, I throw my last seed.

Fruitfulness

Jesus says: "By this is my Father glorified, that you bear much fruit..." (Jn 15:8). He then advises us that it is not enough that we bear much fruit; the fruit must also be lasting: "I appointed you to go and bear fruit that will remain..."(Jn 15:16). What else remains but love? When we shall see God face-to-face, even faith and hope will have run their course; only love is everlasting. It is the risen Jesus who enables us to bear that lasting fruit of love.

Christ "was raised from the dead in order that we might bear fruit for God" (Rom 7:4). In our mission the glorified Christ is present and operative.

Fruitfulness is a paramount biblical concept. Sometimes the lack of fruits is reproved, as in Isaiah's Vineyard Song (5:1-7) or in Jesus' parable of the barren fig tree (Lk 13:6-9). More frequently, however, fruitfulness is extolled. An example of this is the stream of living water flowing from beneath the threshold of the temple. "Wherever the river flows, every sort of living creature that can multiply shall live, and there shall be abundant fish, for wherever this water comes, the sea shall be made fresh...Along both banks of the river, fruit trees of every kind shall grow; their leaves shall not fade, nor their fruit fail. Every month they shall bear fresh fruit, for they shall be watered by the flow from the sanctuary. Their fruit shall serve for food, and their leaves for medicine" (Ez 47:9,12). In the very last chapter of scripture (Rev 22), this eloquent image is taken up again.

Repeatedly in his many parables on the reign of God, Jesus draws comparisons with fruitfulness: the mustard seed, that smallest of all the seeds which, when full grown, is the largest of plants (Mt 13:31-32); the weeds among the wheat (Mt 13:24-30, 36-43); the sower who sows his seed on four different kinds of soil (Mt 13:3-9, 18-23; cf. above). The most telling and convincing image might well be the one of the vine and the branches, which shows how fruitfulness depends completely on the connection between the grapevines and the stem (Jn 15:1-17).

We think we understand. It seems so obvious. To bear fruit means to be productive, to bring to fruition, to achieve, to make a profit. The other side of the coin also makes sense to us: a branch that does not bear fruit is unproductive, hence unprofitable and therefore must be discarded. Without realizing it, however, we interpret the biblical message in the spirit of an achievement society, and in doing so, miss the point. In fact, it is extremely difficult for us honestly to understand what scripture has to say in this regard.

The Achievement Society

The world we live in is permeated with a drive to accomplish and to achieve. That bug is transmitted to us in the very air we breathe. We have all interiorized the basic axiom: "I am what I achieve." In every possible way the performance anxiety is driven home to us day after day. From early childhood it has been instilled in us that everything has to be earned: money, of course, and career, but also recognition, affirmation, gratitude, and, yes, even affection. It would seem that our accomplishments are the only justification for our being alive. Even in old age this achievement obsession does not let us off the hook. The accomplishments are the norm to value ourselves and others. We are trained to ask ourselves constantly: "How do I perform? How do I come across?" The usual greeting, "How are you?" is oftentimes very casual and trite. How seldom is it a serious question. The far more relevant question really is: "What do you do?"

Unfortunately, in the church and in religious life, this unhealthy attitude is not less, but perhaps even more, prevalent than elsewhere. Freud, and even more so his renegade disciple, Adler, could readily explain this tragic phenomenon from their point of view.

In fact, this achievement mentality is so insidious that I would like to cite some examples to illustrate this point.

- Jean Vanier, the founder of "l'Arche," while visiting a classroom in his own country, Canada, noticed a poster with the text, "It is a crime not to excel." It upset him greatly that impressionable children are brainwashed in such a way.
- Many people complain about the vast amount of work, the number of appointments and phone calls, the stack of mail, etc., with which they must contend. Occasionally, though, one gets the impression that they do not want it otherwise. The complaint sounds a little like disguised self-glorification.
- For a person to be able to claim "no time" has become a distinction, because it proves how busy that person is, how much in demand. The concept of "no time" is not looked

upon as a liability as if something were lacking; rather it is construed as a status symbol. Little by little it becomes more appropriate to write it not as two separate words, but rather draw it together into one word: no-time, or notime: an asset.

- In the directory which most religious communities print yearly, the names of all the members are listed as well as their responsibilities and their mission. When old age or an illness calls for retirement, there always remains the meaningful mission "*Orat pro ecclesia et communitate*," i.e., he or she prays for the church and the community. A superior once told me how a father in his nineties fought that assignment. He wanted something more active behind his name.

- Many a sister or brother retiring from office has said to me, "Father, I still want to be of some service." Laudable as this desire may be, the underlying message sometimes can easily be overheard, "I still want to count for something."

- People have a tendency to develop a daily workload or ritual which is somewhat beyond their strength, though realistically this same task could be done more simply. As a result they bring themselves needlessly into a self-imposed stressful situation which provides them with the pleasant feeling of being indispensable. Religious communities are not at all exempt from this tendency, even though this temptation runs counter to the contemplative heart of their lives.

- The most subtle example I came across was in a book by a German Trappist monk,[2] who related the incident of an old brother who confided to his abbot, "The world would be astonished if it would ever know how much wood I have chopped in my life." The sentence is a hypothetical statement in the subjunctive mood. So the brother considers it as an imaginary case; he has accepted the fact that the world will never know about it. Yet, he harbors the secret satisfaction that his achievement in wood-chopping would amaze the world if it would ever be known.

- Accomplishment is by no means always a secret search for profit, recognition, or power. It can very well be a response to a genuine sense of responsibility. Especially people who have an open eye for the needs of others often feel they are called upon explicitly or tacitly to help out. There is something beautiful in this attitude. Yet, even in these cases, things taken on have to be assessed carefully. One's family or community, as well as one's leisure must be safeguarded; a healthy distance must be kept; one's limitations should be heeded; and one's motivation needs to be scrutinized. Let me add from the bottom of my heart that I sincerely hope that these many conditions do not stifle our generosity and desire to help.

Similarities and Differences

There is only a thin line between fruitfulness and achievement. In fact, they overlap, and it would be simplistic to construe a complete opposition between the two. Both fruitfulness and achievement demand effort, discipline and hard work. There is a great deal of labor required to till the land, for it entails plowing and fertilizing, harrowing and sowing, raising and harvesting. Much care, patience and wisdom are needed to grow fruits. It is unarguably true that both fruitfulness and achievement demand toil, each in its own way. Having said this, though, the differences rather than the similarities between the two seem to be more relevant today. I have found at least a dozen of them. They may help us to understand the good news more fully.

10. Room for Mystery

In fruitfulness there is room for mystery. We don't know how
the seed strikes root, shoots up and bears fruit. Moreover, there
is little influence we can have in the process.

> No: it is not yours to open buds into blossoms.
> Shake the bud, strike it; it is beyond your power
>   to make it blossom.
> Your touch soils it, you tear its petals to pieces
>   and strew them in the dust.
> But no colors appear, and no perfumes.
> Ah! It is not for you to open the bud into a blossom.
>
> He who can open the bud does it so simply.
> He gives it a glance, and the life-sap stirs through it veins.
> At his breath the flower spreads its wings and
>   flutters in the wind.
> Colors flush out like heart-longings,
> The perfume betrays a sweet secret.
> He who can open the bud does it so simply![1]

Fruitfulness takes place in hiddenness and trust. Perhaps as a
child we found it hard to believe that the seed would grow and
become a plant; it seemed so unreal to us. So we poked the soil
with our tiny fingers just to check, and in the process destroyed
the seed. Fruitfulness presupposes trust and surrender; it calls
for an open and relaxed attitude. We let happen, let go. An
essential factor is the ability to wait in patience. We are attentive
and involved, yet without control and stress. Jesus illustrates this

attitude in a beautiful little parable when he explains what the reign of God is like (Mk 4:26–29).

> This is how it is with the kingdom of God; it is as if a man were to scatter seed on the land and would sleep and rise night and day and the seed would sprout and grow, he knows not how. Of its own accord the land yields fruit, first the blade, then the ear, then the full grain in the ear. And when the grain is ripe, he wields the sickle at once, for the harvest has come.

Fruitfulness is like a mystery in which we make our home. Contrariwise, the achiever wants to have, as far as humanly possible, everything under control. He or she must pull the strings, so it is indispensable tao have a strong grip on them. Trust, let alone surrender, is out of place in this approach to reality. The five-year planning of the former communist countries are typical examples. Control seems to be the key word here.

When we reflect upon our personal and communal experiences, we soon learn that whoever tries to possess the basic values of life, such as love, friendship, fulfillment, joy, even good health, becomes tense and rigid. "I cannot allow myself a weak moment," a woman said, "or something will go awry." She seemed not to realize that something quite vital had already gone awry, through this very attitude.

Scripture reinforces this human wisdom. Someone who wants to grasp the fruits of the Spirit, like love, joy, peace, or patience (Gal 5:22), loses them. Faith, hope, and love are continually given, but only open hands and open hearts can receive them. In many cases these "divine virtues" are actually powerless; of themselves they yield no immediate tangible advantages. Those who look exclusively or predominantly for profit, diminish the most important dimension of human life.

Jesus in his public life cured many blind, lame and lepers; these healings were meant as signs. Jesus had to fight against the mentality that looked only for utilitarian benefits or worldly profits and not for a genuine faith. "Unless you people see signs and wonders, you will not believe" (Jn 4:48).

Respecting Nature

Fruitfulness is natural and sound. It corresponds to the inherent laws of nature, since all vegetation contains within itself the seed of new life. On the third day of creation God said, "Let the earth bring forth vegetation: every kind of plant that bears seed and every kind of fruit tree on earth that bears fruit with its seed in it" (Gen 1:11). On the sixth day God created all kinds of animals, and as the climax of his creative activity, "God created man in his image...male and female he created them. God blessed them, saying: 'Be fertile and multiply; till the earth and subdue it' · (Gen 1:27–28). Fruitfulness respects the laws of nature and the dignity of the human person.

Achievement often operates at the cost of nature. In recent years it has been painfully brought home to us how the achievement society has been raping the earth for profit. Overcropping, overgrazing, overfishing exhausts the land, the sea, and the rivers. Above all, modern technology is exploiting mother nature beyond her limits, thus mutilating our life-supporting environment of rich soil, clean water, fresh air, and protective ozone. The earth's immune system is damaged. The increasing encroachment on nature unleashes on all nations, not just the poverty-ridden Third World ones, exotic diseases of which AIDS is the most devastating but by no means the only one.

In a similar way, over-accomplishment can ruin a human person. One imposes unhealthy demands on oneself to achieve more than one really can, and after some time is worn out by compulsive competitiveness and fatigue. People feel exhausted, depleted and, contrary to external appearances, devalued. Meanwhile, there looms the terrible threat of burnout. This is certainly not what God had in mind when he found creation "very good"!

Not only the individual, but also the family and the community can be harmed by excessive work. There is not enough leisure just to enjoy each other's company. A genuine interest in the persons with whom we live is eroded. The relentless drive to achieve dampens the relationship between people. By the time we discover how unreasonably high the price is that we pay for a career and success, it is often too late. If only we recognized sooner how devastating such a life-style had become, many a divorce or splitting up of a community could have been avoided.

Likewise the over-emphasis of achievement and competition affects our spiritual life, which is basically communion with God. The relationship with God is almost defenseless in the face of the vehemence of work, work, work. Prayer is such a fragile reality; everything else—work, a visit, a phone call, the news, relaxation—is more imposing than our time spent with God. Precisely because of its fragility, prayer must be protected in a special manner. We are all aware of a baby's frailty; spontaneously we handle it with great care and never place it in such a way that it could possibly be dropped. So, too, our time for prayer has to be given a place where it cannot be dropped. In a world where achievement is the prime value, the spiritual life demands a constant going against the grain.

> The great mystery of fecundity is that it becomes visible where we have given up our attempts to control life and take the risk to let life reveal its own inner movements. Whenever we trust and surrender ourselves to the God of love, fruits will grow. Fruits can only come forth from the ground of intimate love. They are not made, nor are they the result of specific human actions that can be repeated.[2]

Allowing for Flaws

Nature has its flukes and freaks. Not all the fruits which nature produces are prefect. Some may be misshapen or stunted. In the wheat fields weeds will also appear together with the grain. In the reign of God both are allowed to grow until the harvest time (Mt 13:30). Pulling up all the weeds, as the servants suggest, will uproot the wheat as well.

There is profound wisdom in this forbearance. People who impatiently want to establish flawless perfection, do an immense amount of harm to themselves and to others. The history of the church provides us all too numerous examples of fanaticism and cruelty, supposedly in the name of God. Many times the good developed through centuries was wiped out in this way; sometimes the community was split with much pain. Often it was downright violence in a spiritual disguise. The person who cannot tolerate the weeds among the wheat is not inspired by the Spirit of Jesus and not fit for his discipleship. Neither our personal life nor our communities can ever measure up to impeccability. Jesus knew that perfectly well, and incorporated this sound wisdom into the very foundation of his church. When the time for the harvest has come, GOD will be the judge; WE never will be, let alone prematurely.

The spirit of fruitfulness allows for weaknesses and flaws, knowing that God calls us by our name (cf. Is 43:1), which means: as we really are, not as we should be. "You are mine," he says—the whole of you, not just your strengths. Jesus is the perfect image of his Father; as the good shepherd he, too, "calls his own sheep by name and leads them out" (Jn 10:3); again, not just the sheep without blemish (how many of those would he have anyway?) but all of them.

One of those special traits of the gospel is that precisely "in weakness Christ's power is at its best" (2 Cor 12:9, *JB*). In fact, "we know, that *all* things work for good for those who love God" (Rom 8:28). God's tolerance of inadequacy and faults creates an openness in us which perceives and integrates much more than the intransigent person ever does, above all an openness for love and for God.

The performance anxiety focuses completely on strength and potency; it tends to repress all weakness. "I cannot allow myself a weak moment, or something will go awry," the woman said. That is symptomatic. This mentality hankers after results and idolizes efficiency and success. It is highly competitive, fixes itself on the goal to be reached, and pushes aside everything that is in the way, to the point of becoming relentless.

Whenever I happen to swim at a nearby pool on Saturday morning, I always encounter a not-so-young-any-more gentleman who is very determined to do a maximum number of laps in a minimum amount of time. He appears to have no fun whatsoever. It is a grim picture. The vibes send the message: "get out of my way." It strikes me as a symbol of the achievement society. Body signals are overheard, feelings ignored, relationships either neglected or utilized. The drive for competence soon winds up in merciless competition. The whole thrust is so unhealthy! We are not meant to live this way. This is not what the reign of God looks like. God's dream is richer.

In 1145, a onetime monk of the Abbey of Clairvaux was elected pope and took the name Eugene III. At his request, his friend and former abbot, St. Bernard, wrote him a lengthy letter—one may also call it a short treatise—filled with love and concern. This was later followed by four more. One of the first pages zeroes in on the danger of steady overachievement which may lead to a hardened heart. Bernard drives home the point that the pope's calendar must be reduced. The following are some specimens of Bernard's lessons:

> I worry constantly about you. I am afraid that you will be so trapped in your numerous occupations, that you see no way out and therefore harden yourself defiantly; that you suppress little by little the sense of an appropriate and wholesome grief. It is far wiser for you to withdraw from time to time from your affairs than that your affairs draw you and drive you step by step to where you certainly do not want to go. You ask, where? To the point where the heart gets hardened. Do not ask any further what this means. If you are not alarmed now, your heart is already there.

> Those with hardened hearts never attained salvation, unless God had pity on them and took away their hearts of stone and gave them hearts of flesh (cf. Ez 36:26).

> To encompass aptly all the evils of this horrible disease in a single phrase: a hardened heart neither fears God nor respects people (cf. Lk 18:4).

> Look, that is where these cursed activities will drag you if you carry on like this and completely lose yourself to them without

reserving some time and energy for yourself. You waste your time and—if I may allow myself to be for you another Jethro (cf. Ex 18:17–18)—you wear yourself out this way in senseless toil, which only afflicts your mind, eats out your heart and squanders God's grace. What, after all, are the fruits of all this? Are they not mere cobwebs?[3]

11. The Contemplative Dimension

✪

Contemplative in Action

When Henri Nouwen was forty-two years old, he took a leave of absence from Yale Divinity School to spend seven months with the Trappists of Genesee Abbey in upstate New York, where he fully participated in the daily life of the monks. After his first week he wrote the following entry in his diary:

> I'd better start thinking a little more about my attitude toward work. If I have learned anything this week, it is that there is a contemplative way of working that is more important for me than praying, reading, or singing. Most people think that you go to the monastery to pray. Well, I prayed more this week than before but also discovered that I have not learned yet to make the work of my hands into a prayer.

It seems a new and very important discovery for him, so new in fact that he is not yet capable of elaborating on it. Six weeks later, he is able to express himself in more detail:

> If I could slowly come to that trust in God, that surrender, that childlike openness, many tensions and worries would fall away, would be unmasked as false, empty, unnecessary worries, not worth the time and energy, and I could live a simple life. My preaching and teaching, my lecturing and counseling could be like different forms of a meditative life. Then I probably would have

an open mind, open to perceive many things I didn't notice
before, open to hear many people I didn't hear before. Then I
wouldn't worry about my name, my career, my success, my popularity and would be open to the voice of God and his people. Then
I probably also would know much better what is worth doing and
what is not, which lectures to accept and which to refuse, which
people to spend time with and which people to keep at a distance.
Then I most likely would be less plagued by passions causing me
to read the wrong books, hang around the wrong places, and
waste my time with the wrong company. Then—no doubt—I would
have much more time to pray, to read, to study, and to be always
prepared to speak the word of God when the right time has come.
Wherever I am, at home, in a hotel, in a train, plane, or airport, I
would not feel irritated, restless, and desirous of being somewhere
else or doing something else.[1]

What made such a deep impression on Henri Nouwen was the
contemplative element in the work. His entire diary is an eloquent testimony to the fact that monks are by no means slack in
their work; yet, they labor without the pressure which is so typical of most other people who work hard. The labor in the
monastery is performed with the same transparency for God's
presence as prayer is. The more we overcome self-centeredness,
the more we let God's glory shine through. When we are always
intent on building up our ego, we will wind up using even God,
however subtly, to achieve that purpose. The achievement anxiety quenches the contemplative dimension. It is like an engine
with too much friction, which has at least four conspicuous dis-
advantages: eating up much energy, producing little, making a
great deal of noise, and requiring lavish cooling. The same difficulties are experienced by people who put too much of self
into their work. They become opaque.

In a most rewarding conversation with the prior of a
Camaldolese Monastery, I asked him what he felt was the hardest sacrifice in monastic life. He smiled broadly and discarded
some common misconceptions. Then he said quite resolutely,
"In the long run, it is the lack of fulfillment." In the context it
was obvious that he meant the fulfillment flowing from a sense

of achievement. The contemplative life renounces outward success. That is precisely why most outsiders, sometimes even good Catholics, find it hard to accept enclosed monasteries. That is also why, in the course of their history, monastic communities have occasionally been expelled from their countries; yes, even the Carthusians from the Grande Chartreuse: they are not productive in the ordinary sense of the word. In this respect they are true followers of Jesus, who met with basically the same difficulty. He preached the God of love and the love of God. But love is in itself not profitable. Eventually Jesus disappointed all those who sought only tangible results. Success was not characteristic of Jesus.

If the monk and the nun remain faithful in their renunciation of success and deepen this attitude, their work becomes prayer. The transparency of selflessness bridges the gap between contemplation and action; over the years the two become one.

Whoever strives to be contemplative in action has to meet the same condition. It is undoubtedly a sublime ideal, but the price is high and is not to be paid in any foreign currency, but with our innermost treasure. We have to overcome our selfishness and our subtle self-seeking. It is not so much *what* we do, but rather *why* and *how* we do it, that can make our activity into a sacred place in which God is allowed to be present and active and in charge. As with the monks, this does not mean that we produce less, but that we work in a selfless way. Such a manner of working is a precious service to our contemporaries. It would be such a blessing if people do not have to travel to Genesee Abbey or a similar monastery to experience work that has become prayer. The example of activity in union with contemplation might, in fact, well be more important than all our work can possibly produce. Isn't that the help many people are searching for, sometimes even as far as India or Japan?

Gratuity

For Ignatius and his first companions the gratuity of their ministry was of vital importance. It is mentioned immediately in the first paragraph of the first sketch of the Constitutions to come (called the "Formula of the Institute") and then repeated over and over again. The first Jesuits had experienced how the clergy's avidity for material profit did tremendous damage to the apostolate. Because of this, entire areas of ministry were neglected. This example of greed did more harm to the faith of the people than all the good which words could possibly effect. The "friends in the Lord" recognized gratuity of ministry as a radical means for a reform of the church in head and members, since it would attack the evil at its very root.

Gratuity, however, is much more than just a way to remedy the apostolic ministry, no matter how important the latter may be. In the gospel, gratuity is based far more deeply than in ministerial improvement. It is a basic attitude in the following of Jesus: "Without cost you have received; without cost you are to give" (Mt 10:8). Though the 31st and 32nd General Congregations (1965 and 1974/75) loosened the canonical form of the gratuity somewhat in order to account for the shift in the meaning of earning and begging, our apostolate remains as before rooted in the evangelical gratuity, which extends far beyond the realm of finances.

Not just our ability and our talents, but our whole life is a gratuitous gift from God. God has loved us unconditionally into being. This priority of the divine love is the ultimate basis of our existence. We don't have to earn the justification of our life by our achievements. Our life has been given to us undeservedly and freely. God's love, which is the origin of our life, cannot be earned; neither can it be lost. It has no conditions. It takes its measure from itself, not from us, not to mention from our productivity.

Gratuity renders our life transparent so that its source can come through. Gratuity is the down-to-earth way of showing that our life is free, that it is a pure gift without calculation, a gift just because God finds joy in our being. Because it is a mere gift, we in turn shall also freely give: gratuity.

In 1992 the German bishops published a pastoral letter on priestly ministry, mainly to encourage the priests at a time in which their service is becoming more and more difficult. The bishops pointed out this vital dimension of the apostolate: "The effectiveness of the priestly mission depends on its gratuitousness, which does not look for recompense or success. 'Fruits' do not grow on command, but normally by themselves."[2]

It is freeing when in our ministry and in our faith we are not anxious for results. It is not the numbers that count. Of course, there is gratification in reaching many people and we may enjoy this when it happens to be the case, but let us not build on it. It is not necessary to be relevant at all costs. To live and celebrate our faith makes a great deal of sense even when we are only a small minority and never adequately live up to the gospel. That is the way to bear much fruit, though we ourselves will never be able to assess it properly.

Living life in a spirit of gratuity touches a deep desire in every human heart. In a society which is so unsparingly geared toward accomplishment, and which cares about the individual only insofar as he or she is profitable, there is still a strong need in each of us to be appreciated for what we are, not just for what we achieve. The gratuitousness of our being created remains alive in us as a deep longing that cannot be satisfied in accomplishments only, no matter how successful they may be. We all want to count for more than what we produce. To show the people of today how to assuage this hunger is a prime service of any ministry.

People who ignore this basic human need and try to live only on their achievements are heading for disaster. Sooner or later our ability to achieve will diminish or perhaps cease completely. The person who has identified solely with work then tumbles into an identity crisis. If there is no deeper level to fall back upon, the crisis is total and life becomes meaningless. It is sad to witness the breakdown of people, some of whom had been extremely successful. Once their activity ceased, it was too late to change their basic attitude. Old age is revealing for everything that went before. When through our way of life and our words we help prevent such havoc, if only for a few people, we have effected much good.

The achievement society applauds those who have attained great success, especially when they started at the bottom of the ladder. But the same system is merciless to those who, according to its standards, have not succeeded. Idolizing accomplishments, like any worship of idols, is dehumanizing. Notwithstanding all social security, our society can be ruthless toward those it deems to be failures. For these people gratuity is a very important signal that can give more meaning to their lives.

Gratuity not only discloses our human life as a free gift, but also reveals to us that God is a giving God, to the point of giving even his very self (Sp Ex 234: *Deus communicans*). The mystery of the blessed Trinity is nothing but self-giving: the Father, who gives himself completely to his Son and the Son who in return surrenders himself to the Father unreservedly; the Holy Spirit, who is bond and gift, not as some*thing* but as Some*one*. This circle of self-giving is the source of all love and therefore of all life. The whole of creation is but an echo of this trinitarian mystery, the fruit of God's continuous self-giving. Gratuity tries to keep this self-giving accessible in a world that is on the way to blocking it out.

Like the Grain of Wheat

In an extremely powerful and unadorned image, Jesus accentuates a basic law of all fruitfulness: "Amen, amen, I say to you, unless a grain of wheat falls to the ground and dies, it remains just a grain of wheat; but if it dies, it produces much fruit" (Jn 12:24). Of course, not only fecundity, but also accomplishment costs; yet this unpalatable rule of giving up self is not usually promoted by the achievement society; in fact, it runs counter to its basic tenet.

The gospel, on the contrary, teaches: "Whoever wishes to save his life will lose it, but whoever loses his life for my sake will find it. What profit would there be for one to gain the whole world and forfeit one's life? Or what can one give in exchange for one's life?" (Mt 16:25–26). Not only did Jesus preach this life and death wisdom, but he also lived it. It constitutes the core of his whole existence: the paschal mystery. The entire gospel finds its center in the unbreakable unity of the death and resurrection of Jesus; everything the gospel tells us should be read in the light of this core mystery. "By this is my Father glorified, that you bear much fruit." In order to do so we have to remain in Jesus' love. But there, in his love, we will share in the mystery that holds his whole life and mission together: the paschal mystery.

In a somewhat different perspective, Rabindranath Tagore shares with us a similar deep insight: "My life when young was like a flower—a flower that loosens a petal or two from her abundance and never feels the loss when the spring breeze comes to beg at her door. Now at the end of youth my life is like a fruit, having nothing to spare, and waiting to offer herself completely with her full burden of sweetness."[3]

This unselfish surrender forms the completion of our life whereby it yields a rich harvest. Once again it is God who works in us this ultimate surrender. Scripture never tires of repeating the preeminence of God's activity in and beyond our action. In a sweeping statement St. Paul says: "There are different workings but the same God who produces all of them in everyone" (1 Cor 12:6).

The more we interiorize that God is working in our work, the more that peace will grow in us which the world can neither give nor take away, and the more we shall be peacemakers in this very special sense of the word. It will free us from the pressure to base our self-esteem on our accomplishments. This, in turn, will cause us to posit different priorities and to choose different activities; and above all, to perform these activities in a different way. Jesus said to his disciples: "It was not you who chose me, but I who chose you and appointed you to go and to bear fruit that will remain" (Jn 15:16). To live this way means to cease focusing on our achievements. Is not this an essential element of the alternative life-style about which so many people speak nowadays?

12. In a Genuine Relationship

Compensation

Fruitfulness presupposes a relationship. It always implies receptiveness, i.e., the ability to receive, to let oneself be affected. This law of nature already holds in the vegetative sphere. Unless plants are fertilized, they cannot bear fruit. It is typical of our technological age that the word "to fertilize" has become ambiguous. Many people will spontaneously picture a chemical substance used as artificial manure. In our context, of course, the word means the coming together of a male and female gamete which brings forth the fruit. Since plants cannot move around, a bee or another insect has to establish the relationship, without which there cannot be any fruit.

With the animals it is even more obvious that fruitfulness presupposes a relationship. And so it is with people. And then the reign of God is also all about relationships, ones that are intimate and lasting. The most impelling comparison is that of the vine with its branches. It is the life-giving sap of the vine flowing through the branches which enables them to bear fruit. Apart from the vine, the branch cannot bear fruit. Similarly, "cut off from me," Jesus says, "you can do nothing" (Jn 15:5), with the self-evident implication: "Nothing worthwhile for the reign of God." Of course, cut off from Jesus we can certainly achieve quite a lot; but that is not bearing any fruit for the reign of God.

Undoubtedly there are people who accomplish much, yet bear little fruit; just as there are people who accomplish little, but are very fruitful. Think of Mary, the most fruitful person of our race, since Jesus was the fruit of her womb; yet she did not achieve much. A good question is: how do we measure people?

Achievement can be a substitute for a lack of true relationships. Because we do not find the human fulfillment which only an authentic relationship can give, we try to substitute enormous accomplishments in its place.

Our life with all its activities can only be fruitful in the biblical sense, if we let God's action come through in our human action. This means that while we are active, we are at the same time receptive for God's initiative. In the Spiritual Exercises, St. Ignatius says, "We must allow God to put into our soul what we ought to do" (Sp Ex 180). It is this combination of activity and receptivity, of our own effort and our being led, that constitutes the secret of fruitfulness and which the achievement mentality tends to undo. In following Jesus we begin to realize more and more that all that is being asked from us has in a way already been accomplished (Hermann Bezzel).

We Are God's Co-Workers (1 Cor 3:9)

The human person in both the Old and the New Testaments is characterized as having great dignity. Though "formed out of the clay of the ground" (Gen 2:7, Adam stems from *adamah*, which is the Hebrew word for soil), man and woman are "made little less than a god, crowned with glory and honor" (Ps 8:6). The crown of glory and honor consists, according to the psalm, in the fact that "you, God, gave them power over the works of your hand and put all things under their feet" (8:7). They are to cooperate with the creative activity of the creator. On the sixth day of creation God said "Let us make man in our image, after our likeness" (Gen 1:26). What it means for human beings to be made in the image and likeness of God is explained immediately afterwards; it consists again primarily in their governing the rest of creation. They are to care for the world in partnership with God and as representatives of God. "Let them have dominion over the fish of the sea, the birds of the air, and the cattle, and over all the wild animals and all the creatures that crawl on the ground. God created man in his image, in the divine image he created him; male and female he created them" (Gen 1:26–27). Then the second account of the creation, shaped in the Yahwistic tradition, vividly depicts this human stewardship in the parade of the various animals before *ha'adam* "to see what he would call them; whatever *ha'adam* called each of them would be its name" (Gen 2:19). Hence this name-giving sovereignty enlists all animals in the service and responsibility of humankind. It makes our world into a divine-human workshop. The human person is the co-creator of the earth. In the fourth eucharistic prayer we say, "You formed man and woman in your own likeness and set them over the whole world to serve you, their creator, and to rule over all creatures."

There is an attractive commentary in the Talmud on the word "us" in the verse, "Let *us* make man in our image, after our likeness" (Gen 1:26). The Rabbi asked, "With whom did God speak when he said 'us'?" A Christian might spontaneously think of the blessed Trinity yet that answer is not a part of Jewish tradition. The Rabbi answered his own question: "God already spoke with the human person yet to be created. You and I together, we shall create the human person. Because if you do not cooperate, I can never make you into a right and proper person." We are not just passive beneficiaries, but privileged partners.

Indeed, from a biblical perspective we are the shapers and builders, not only of our world but also of our own lives. We are free agents; we may let the world and ourselves go one way or another, and thus we determine the direction in which history may go.

In the third chapter, the book of Genesis describes the traumatic scene, in which man and woman grab beyond their scope. Adam and Eve turn away from their cooperation with the creator and attempt their own independent dominion. Their rebellion backfires into a curse because they impose too heavy a burden on themselves, and cannot of themselves do justice to the world. Exactly the same work which is considered paradisal in Genesis

2:15 (to cultivate the land), becomes a punishment after the fall, causing much sweat and labor (Gen 3:23). The banishment from the garden of Eden does not mean that Adam and Eve have to go to another place, but rather that they cut themselves off from divinely-sponsored fruitfulness and condemn themselves to the curse of self-achievement and the load of ultimate responsibility.

In the last chapter of the primeval history (Gen 11), humankind commits again the same sin. In the construction of the tower of Babel, they try to blot out the boundary between heaven and earth by means of achieving something monumental. Again they overburden themselves and fail miserably. They, who wanted "to make a name for themselves," are scattered into the isolation of confused languages.

In the next chapter salvation history begins with Abram, who leaves his home and his kinsfolk and as a migrant receives from God a new name. God gives him a promise and a blessing, so that in turn he himself will be a blessing for many. In this way the labor of Abraham is reinserted into the work of God, and thus rendered abundantly fruitful. Abraham is the antipode of the achiever. He is the father of all believers.

Ignatius likes the image of the instrument to express our collaboration in God's work. It conveys that in the work of salvation (and the great passion of Ignatius *iuvare animas* i.e., to help the souls, is a work of salvation), all activity has its origin in the Holy One and is received from God, who gives it to us gratuitously. We are partners with the ultimate source of all good. We are responsible, but do not have the final responsibility. We are instruments in God's hands. Our joy is to fit perfectly into God's craftsmanship and to be as compliant as can be. We may be sure that we, as God's instruments, will be used with the greatest care and regard, affinity and delight, just as violinists use their violins.

Faith vs. Law

One of the most important issues for Paul was that our salvation comes through faith and not through the law. It is the main theme of Romans, his longest and most significant letter. Also, he passionately deals with the same topic in his letter to the Galatians. To those who are not familiar with biblical theology, this fierce discussion may seem strange. Today, perhaps the antithesis might be translated with the words fruitfulness and achievement, and thus be more relevant.

Righteousness and holiness are essential qualities of God; so much so that they are considered names of God. God graciously bestows these qualities on us, thus changing our innermost being. The irreducible distinction, however, is and will always remain, that God is just and holy by his very nature, while we are justified and sanctified, not of our own strength, but by God.

The great temptation of the law is that we strive to assure our salvation by strict observance of the law. Our drive for achievement then intrudes into the exclusively divine pale, overstepping its own domain. The interiorized maxim, "I am what I achieve," when applied to faith and the relation with God, is completely out of place here and far more devastating than in any other sphere. The law provokes the self-centered person to illusory superaccomplishments, attempting to usurp God's place. "You will be like gods," was the serpent's wording of the fundamental temptation. Such an attitude strives to reduce God to an entity confined to our world.

Those who think and live this way pervert the law; they use it as an instrument to achieve their salvation. This mentality can never bring the freedom of the children of God, but leads to the subjection under a strenuous taskmaster, who can never be pleased. "All who depend on works of the law are under a curse," Paul writes (Gal 3:10). It is the pinnacle of the performance anxiety and a radical self-deception as well.

Our receptiveness for God's grace releases us from the compulsion of self-deification and the superhuman burden which is a part of it. Graciously we share in the divine life, something which we can never effect ourselves. God introduces us into the mystery of the triune life and love of Father, Son and Holy Spirit. It is Jesus who enables us to have our dwelling place where he himself is at home and secure. "To those who did accept him he gave power to become children of God" (Jn 1:12). The key is our openness to God's freely-given grace, for then the life of God can develop and bear fruit in us. With Paul we, too, will be able to say one day, "By the grace of God I am what I am, and his grace to me has not been fruitless" (1 Cor 15:10). It is not our activity which justifies us, rather our justification activates us (Wilfried Joest).

The dividing line between grace and law is like the turning point which separates the working out of fulfillment from the working out of need. The latter is a pressurized effort to procure relief and gain; it is characterized by an agonizing anxiety. The former, however, operates from a sense of contentment, freely spreading its bounty.

13. Living the Covenant

I Tell You, Not to Worry

I tell you, do not worry about your life, what you will eat or drink, or about your body, what you will wear. Is not life more than food and the body more than clothing? Look at the birds in the sky; they do not sow or reap, they gather nothing into barns, yet your heavenly Father feeds them. Are not you more important than they? Can any of you by worrying add a single moment to your life-span? Why are you anxious about clothes? Learn from the way the wild flowers grow. They do not work or spin. But I tell you that not even Solomon in all his splendor was clothed like one of them. If God so clothes the grass of the field, which grows today and is thrown into the oven tomorrow, will he not much more provide for you, O you of little faith? So do not worry and say, "What are we to eat?" or "What are we to drink?" or "What are we to wear?" All these things the pagans seek. Your heavenly Father knows that you need them all. But seek first the kingdom of God and its righteousness, and all these things will be given you besides (Mt 6:25–33).

"Your heavenly Father knows that you need all these things." He also knows that we need more than just clothes and food and drink; we also need security, belonging, acceptance, success, fulfillment, sympathy, and love. All these vital values come to us through people; our heavenly Father works through them.

We certainly have to provide and plan ahead for "all these things." But Jesus forbids us to worry anxiously about them. While making preparations, we must at the same time rely on

God's loving care. Such reliance releases us from anxiety. These things should neither be the prime motivation in our work nor the determining factor in our decisions. "Seek first God's kingdom and its righteousness"—which means a moral conduct in conformity with God's plan for the salvation of humankind—"and all these things will be given you besides," including such things as recognition and affection and the like. When we receive them, let us do so wholeheartedly, let us enjoy and savor them gladly. Yet let us also acknowledge the Almighty as their origin and give thanks to God. "Nothing is to be rejected when received with thanksgiving, for it is made holy by the invocation of God in prayer" (1 Tim 4:4–5). That means that we do not anxiously cling to these gifts as if we have to defend them against God snatching them away from us. Gratitude, like gratuity, renders us transparent; both let the origin shine through and liberate us from undue stress.

In his comparison with the birds and flowers, Jesus basically does nothing but present the covenant in a new way. Its essence has always been that we seek God with all our heart, and with all our soul, and with all our strength; and that God will take care of us. It is a shift of focus, an exchange of the centers of gravity. *We* make God our priority, and *God* makes our well-being the divine concern. Each cares for the other rather than for self. That instills in us a great relief and a deep satisfaction. There is certainly no less ardor than before, but now it is a concern for the covenant-partner, so the sting of selfishness is gone. That makes all the difference in the world! As the worries are blown away, great simplicity of life surges. God makes sure that we have all we need to sustain our body and mind and heart. Granted, there will be desert periods from time to time, when we feel depleted and forgotten. These, too, belong to the covenant. Without such experiences we would become too complacent and slip out of the covenant. They also have a meaning. Human nature being what it is, they are even needed—for our purification; we are consoled to know that "all things work for good for those who love God" (Rom 8:28). Everything is taken up into the covenant. And God guarantees that the trials will not be beyond our strength (cf. 1 Cor 10:13).

It is easy to write or read this for those who belong to the 20 percent of the world's population who consume 80 percent of the earth's resources. Yet the covenant is also meant for the other 80 percent of humankind. God cares for them as much as he does for us, and he wants to extend his care through us. That is again the concept (or rather, reality) of mission: God being present and active in the person he sends. No covenant without mission! And part of that mission in the western world is, without any doubt, that we finally manage to find ways to share our abundance with those who hunger and starve.

The covenant is fruitful to the degree that, with great trust in God, we diligently commit ourselves to our mission. The Hungarian Jesuit, Gabriel Hevenesi (†1715), summarized some thoughts of St. Ignatius in the ingenious saying:

> Let your first rule of action be,
> to trust in God,
> as if success depended entirely on yourself
> and not on God;
> yet use all your efforts
> as if you yourself did nothing
> and God alone everything.[1]

Fittingly, he does not say: *although* we have to act ourselves, we still have to trust in God, but: *because*...Our ability, both in its strength and in its weakness, always refers to him, whose power is effective in it. Again: not *although* God works everything, we are still supposed to act, but *because* he works everything—in us and through us. One could also say: Undertake all you do with care, as God would do it. Do the works of God.

How do we know that we truly do this? The sign is that spiritual consolation grows; i.e., that our relationship with God becomes more intimate, and that faith, hope and love increase (cf. Sp Ex 316). Our hearts warm, and peace expands.

Not to be Displayed

Unlike the harvest of the field or the orchard, the fruitfulness in God's kingdom often cannot be measured. Usually it remains not assessable and hidden, known only to the Almighty, "who sees in secret" (Mt 6:4, 6, 18). It gives glory to the One who "caused the growth" (1 Cor 3:6). Achievement, on the contrary, can be exhibited and magnify our own glory and honor. It is tangible and quantifiable, it proves our worth.

In German there is a popular proverb which says: "Who counts, forfeits the blessing." To bless is to affirm and foster life. God's blessing has the power to bestow growth, fruitfulness and fruition. The unadorned faith, deposited in the common language, knows that counting can shift the balance and deprive one of the blessing.

At the very end of his life, David exemplifies in a tragic way how this can happen. It is a curious, and at first sight eerie example, which illustrates the evil of being too self-reliant; at the same time it brings home to us forcibly, how much we usually are taken up by the spirit of our accomplishments, and how different the perspective of scripture is.

When David was old and feeble, he ordered a census in Israel and Judah so as to measure his strength (2 Sam 24). The commander-in-chief, Joab, objected: "May Your God, the Most High, increase the number of people a hundredfold for your royal majesty to see it with his own eyes. But why does it please my lord the king to order a thing of this kind?" The king, however, insisted, and overruled his general. So the census was taken and Joab reported to David the number of people registered: in Israel eight hundred thousand men were fit for military service and in Judah, five hundred thousand. Then the king realized his fault; he prayed to God: "I have sinned grievously in what I have done. But now, O God, forgive the guilt of your servant, for I have been very foolish." Nevertheless, this sin is punished severely before it is forgiven.

We wonder: what for heaven's sake is David's guilt in the case? The question becomes even more pressing, when we remember that during the journey through the desert, Moses on two occasions had a census taken—as recorded in chapters 1 and 26 of the book of Numbers; in fact, the book derives its name from these two censuses. They were taken on divine command, near the beginning and toward the end of the desert experience, and clearly had a religious significance.

It is obvious that a census is in itself not sinful. Why, then, is it such a grievous offense in David's case?

The answer is to be found in the origin of David's call. He had been chosen as a young boy while he was tending his father Jesse's sheep, after Samuel had rejected his seven elder brothers one by one. His first major experience of God came soon afterwards, in his fight with Goliath. David had stated his position clearly when he said to the Philistine giant: "You come against me with a sword and spear and scimitar, but I come against you in the name of the Most High God" (1 Sam 17:45). In "the last words of David" (2 Sam 23), he expresses once more how God had always held him: "Is not my house firm before God? He has made an eternal covenant with me, set forth in detail and secured" (v 5). And now while the time has come for David to prepare himself to leave everything behind, he ignores his life-long experience of God and starts counting his strength. But had not God always been his strength? Is this sudden display of power, therefore, not a lack of trust in the reliability of God which had been so unmistakably evident throughout his long life?

Once David needed the prophet Nathan to help him face the sin he had committed with Bathsheba and against Uriah (2 Sam 12). This time his own conscience reacts more quickly and with greater sensitivity. The prophet Gad has only to confirm that and to announce God's sentence. This incident can open our eyes to see the breach of confidence which can be hidden in the display of our accomplishments, and to realize how sensitive God is to that way of thinking.

Until Death

The older we become, the more our accomplishments diminish. For a professional athlete this experience usually comes fairly early in life, but if we live long enough each of us discovers it in our own way. Our body and mind slow down. Fruitfulness, on the other hand, can increase with the number of years. Several psalms proclaim this joyfully and gratefully, e.g., "The just will flourish like the palm-tree and grow like a Lebanon cedar. Planted in the house of the Lord, they will flourish in the courts of our God, still bearing fruit when they are old, still full of sap, still green, to proclaim that the Lord is just" (Ps 92: 13–16).

The decline of our ability is clearly one of the trials we must come to terms with as we age. It is not easy. The drive to stay young is sound and normal. Obviously, the public opinion in the western world strongly fosters this hankering. There is much good in this tendency and it brings a genuine fulfillment. Yet, this drive can sometimes be pushed to extremes and become unhealthy. A youth mystique is biased against senior citizens. And some of the elderly themselves get so engrossed in this climate of opinion that they become obsessed with staying young and "with it," terrified by the dread of age. It then becomes a repression of reality; so much energy is put into denying the obvious, that it is almost humorous, if it were not so distressful to them. A spirituality of fruitfulness could relieve these people of their grim anxiety. When so many believing people (including religious) suffer keenly from the decline of their accomplishments, one wonders whether the achievement society has not overly infected them. Might there not be a too narrow understanding of what it means to be relevant?

It is not only the elderly who wrestle with this problem. There are people who are admirable in faithfully visiting the aged and the sick. But there are others who consistently avoid these visits, to the point of being insensitive. Apparently they find it hard to visit the elderly. There may be several reasons for this reluctance. The confrontation with debilitation is undoubtedly one of them. Inevitably it brings home to them that they, too, may some day experience a similar decline. The fear for our own diminishment easily can lead to repression. There may be plenty of excuses put forth. Yet it is a pity.

The danger of evaluating and ranking people according to very secondary criteria looms greatly in the achievement society.

Some people are interesting because they enrich us in our intellectual, affective, emotional, erotic, culinary, financial, or whatever, realm. Others gratify our helper syndrome and thus enhance our feeling of self-worth. The gospel challenges us to go beyond these rather selfish categories and to love our neighbor as ourself, any neighbor.

A priest in his eighties expressed this wish: "I ardently desire that the last stretch of my life's journey will be a period of deep love for God and selfless service to the world. It is wonderful that with advancing age the awareness of being missioned seems to deepen. It certainly becomes more and more an invisible service, unnoticed also by "my old self" (Col 3:9), and therefore all the more unselfish—completely hidden in the love of Christ. I pray often that God may purify me in this service of mine for the great encounter."

14. An Example of St. Francis

Crippled from birth, a brother,[1] who could move only laboriously with the help of crutches, lived in a monastery in Bologna. He was extremely efficient in making baskets which were in great demand. Weekly he would offer them at the market in exchange for foodstuffs so that he could contribute to the support of the community. One day St. Francis visited the monastery. The brother recounted with joyous enthusiasm how much the people wanted his baskets, and that despite all his endeavors he could never produce enough.

Francis sighed, looked at him and said, "How easily do the weapons fighting on the side of God turn into weapons fighting on the side of sin (cf. Rom 6:13). Though we live in this world, we do not fight with the weapons of this world. The weapons which we use in our holy battle, are not of the flesh (cf. 2 Cor 10:3–4), but are our holy vows."

"Exalted is holy poverty, if it adorns all our works with humility. Radiant is chastity, if our light shines for the people in such a way that because of our works they praise our Father in heaven. Precious is holy obedience, if we let the measure of our work be given to us and do not snatch it ourselves."

The brother, shaken and filled with remorse, confessed to St. Francis the pride, lack of obedience, and self-righteousness which possessed his heart. Francis thereupon embraced him tenderly, blessed him, and said: "Whatever we begin needs the sanctification through our prayer; therefore, go in prayer to God to whom alone your heart belongs before performing what you are told to do. Let your mind be filled with his love and strengthened by his Holy Spirit; then your works will bring forth fruits of the Spirit (cf. Gal 5:22). That is the only way to escape the danger of our well-intentioned deeds turning into works of the flesh and of the darkness" (cf. Gal 5:19–2), Rom 13:12–13).

The brother thanked St. Francis. From then on he made his baskets as vessels of the precious treasure of God's love, and filled them with prayer and blessings for the people.

The message of the story climaxes in the fact that the brother continues to do the same work as he had done before, but in a different spirit. The work which used to be full of self is transformed; it is now full of God.

V

DWELLING IN UNAPPROACHABLE LIGHT

15. The Inexhaustible Mystery

The priest was young, about twenty-five. He was celebrating the liturgy in the temple as IT happened: in an overwhelming experience, God broke most unexpectedly into his life. Undoubtedly, he had been a devout man from his youth, yet in no way was he prepared for this encounter with the overpowering splendor of God. Suddenly he found himself face-to-face with the Holy One. It was shattering. He sensed deeply his absolute unworthiness, his being completely out of place. He felt as insignificant as dust and ashes. He lost his grip and tumbled helplessly into the abysmal chasm between creator and creature, between the All Holy and the sinner. He was overawed by this encounter, a perfectly healthy reaction.

Not even Moses "whom God selected from all humankind for his trustworthiness and meekness" (Sir 45:4), was holy enough to bear the glory of God almighty: "Moses could not enter the meeting tent, because the cloud settled down upon it and the glory of the Most High filled the Dwelling" (Ex 40:35). Previously, in a quite difficult predicament, Moses had been warned unequivocally of his unsuitability to see God: "You can-not see my face, for no human being sees me and still lives" (Ex 33:20). And now young Isaiah—that was the priest's name—is, without any preparation or warning, confronted with God's majesty. Yet, can ever any warning or preparation be the least bit adequate for this experience of divine majesty? When many

years later Isaiah puts this shattering encounter into words, his
account is still full of vibrations:

> In the year King Uzziah died, I saw the Lord seated on a high and
> lofty throne, with the train of his garment filling the temple.
> Seraphim were stationed above; each of them had six wing; with
> two they veiled their faces, with two they veiled their feet, and
> with two they hovered aloft.
>
> "Holy, holy, holy is the LORD of hosts!" they cried one to the
> other. "All the earth is filled with his glory!" At the sound of that
> cry, the frame of the door shook and the house was filled with
> smoke.
>
> Then I said, "Woe is me, I am doomed! For I am a man of unclean
> lips, living among a people of unclean lips; yet my eyes have seen
> the King, the LORD of hosts!" Then one of the seraphim flew to
> me, holding an ember which he had taken with tongs from the
> altar.
>
> He touched my mouth with it. "See," he said, "now that this has
> touched your lips, your wickedness is removed, your sin purged"
> (Is 6:1–7).

Kabod

In Hebrew language the Bible uses a special word to point out
the extraordinary reality at stake: *kabod*. The word is strange to
us, not just because of the foreign language, but even more so
because of its bewildering content. That content is especially per-
plexing to us, and modern preaching rarely risks the topic. The
most profitable approach to grasp its meaning is not an intellectual analysis, but rather an interior savoring. After all, we are
not dealing here with a problem to be solved, but with a mystery
to which we must open up. Mystery can be described negatively
as a reality which we can never adequately understand, or positively as a reality into which our understanding penetrates ever

more deeply. There the heart makes more headway than the intellect; meditation is more helpful than discussion.

In Hebrew the word *kabod* has a threefold meaning. First, it means the weight of something, the heaviness which is measured on a scale. This is the literal sense of the word. Often, however, *kabod* is used figuratively, indicating the prominence of a person. In our language we would use the expression VIP. Joseph, who had risen to vice-king of Egypt, is an example from scripture. He sends his brothers back to their father, Jacob, with the message: "Tell my father all about my high position (*kabod*) in Egypt and what you have seen" (Gen 45:13).

Then there is still a third meaning of the word *kabod*, which in the Bible is undoubtedly the most important one. Here it denotes the "weight," greatness, eminence, power and authority of God. Time and time again scripture stresses that God is invisible. The manifestation of God's grandeur in which yet God's very self remains hidden, is what the Jews call *kabod*. Eventually the word *kabod* ranks as a proper name for God. The *kabod* is the Most High, revealing the divine power and majesty to people while yet remaining incomprehensible. The *kabod* secures God's hiddenness and pronounces at the same time God's (very restricted) self-revelation, God's perceived presence. Similarly, the holiest name of all, YHWH, signifies God's presence, but not God's essence: it assures that God is with us, without telling us who God is. The name *kabod* conveys the unapproachable majesty and power of God.

This divine *kabod* is by no means static, as our explanation so far might wrongly suggest; on the contrary, it is extremely dynamic and effective. It works the great marvels of God, the greatest of which in the Old Testament is the crossing of the Red Sea. From generation to generation the people sing of God's miraculous power that performed these wonders. It is an incomparable force with which nothing can compete. The word *kabod* also carries the connotation of dazzling light, which blinds our sight and which the eyes of no creature can possibly behold. God's *kabod* flashes out as mighty lightning, experienced by us as darkness by its excess of brilliant light. We cannot bear the fiery radiance of divine holiness which we call *kabod*, far less than we can face the sun in its full force. "To Israelites the glory (*kabod*) of God was seen as a consuming fire on the mountaintop" (Ex 24:17).

> A quality of holiness, a quality of power,
> A quality of fearfulness, a quality of sublimity,
> A quality of trembling, a quality of shaking,
> A quality of terror, a quality of consternation,
> Is the quality of the Garment of Zoharariel, YHWH,
>   God of Israel,
> Who comes crowned to the Throne of His Glory...
> And of no creature are the eyes able to behold it,
> Not the eyes of flesh and blood, and not the eyes
>   of His servants.
> And as for him who does behold it, or sees or
>   glimpses it,
> Whirling gyrations grip the balls of his eyes,
> And the balls of his eyes...send forth torches of fire,
> And these enkindle him and these burn him...[1]

That God is unapproachable for us humans, is not due to our sinfulness, nor to a kind of reluctance on God's part, nor is it a provisional circumstance, which a gradual self-revelation of God or a growing holiness on our part will clear up more and more. God is and remains absolute mystery. It is proper to God to transcend all we know or say about the Holy One.

God is inexpressibly other, absolutely incomparable. St. Augustine puts it pithily: *Si comprehendis, non est Deus*—If you have understood, then what you have understood is not God.[2] This is also true for the angels. In Isaiah's vision, the seraphs cover their faces with two wings so as not to see the Holy One. For them, too, God is incomprehensible and inaccessible.

What Isaiah experienced in the year King Uzziah died was precisely this *kabod*: the glorious majesty of God and the endless honor due to the Almighty. The *kabod* has stamped the life of the prophet once and for all. He has never outgrown this encounter. He will always speak about God as the One who is three times holy and powerful. Isaiah will also never lose the awareness of human inappropriateness.

This *kabod* permeates not only the book of Isaiah, but the whole Bible: "Terrible and awesome are you, stronger than the ancient mountains" (Ps 76:5). It impregnates the liturgy of both the Old and the New Testaments. The "holy, holy, holy" in our eucharists reminds us each time of the vision that constituted the call of Isaiah. The "Glory to the Father and to the Son and to the Holy Spirit," which punctuates our praying the psalms, is a human response to the divine *kabod*. Our worship certainly does not add anything to God's *kabod*, as one of our prefaces (the fourth for weekdays) states explicitly: "You have no need of our praise...our prayer of thanksgiving adds nothing to your greatness..."; but for us it is a necessity. Whoever has brushed the divine *kabod*, cannot but adore God.[3]

To Praise God

St. Ignatius requires in the "Principle and Foundation" of his Spiritual Exercises the attitude that "we desire and choose only that which is more conducive to the end for which we are created."[4] This end he described a little earlier in the same paragraph as: "to praise, reverence and serve God our Lord and by this means to save our soul" (Sp Ex 23). "The greater service and praise of the Divine Majesty" (Sp Ex 183) is always pivotal for him.

This "praise of the Divine Majesty" can easily be taken too lightly. We set foot here into a realm which today often has little meaning and not even the proper vocabulary. Yet we deal with something that is essential for religion and faith. Consequently, we have to be a little counter-cultural. That is not a pleasant experience, yet it is not new either. From the first century on, the faithful have been going against the grain.

There is no need to be bashful. If we genuinely communicate what God revealed to us in scripture and tradition, and if we do so as far as possible in today's idiom, we shall find that we answer many people's questions. What seemed untimely has often brought the response to what the prevalent market did not cater for, provided it was authentic. So many in our day search for the beyond with great efforts and sacrifices. They quest the holy, though they may use other words for it. There has been a shift from religious and theological language to psychological and sociological paradigms, but the underlying hunger cannot be assuaged without genuine faith. Our mission may not be easy and popular, but relevant it is!

Whoever has only a slight feeling of the abyss between divine *kabod* and human insufficiency, between God's holiness and our sinfulness, and who also senses somewhat that this abyss cannot be bridged, will experience something that is difficult to describe, and yet is vitally important. Isaiah said: "Woe is me, I am doomed" (6:5), and Peter cried out, "Depart from me, Lord, for I am a sinful man" (Lk 5:8). The word "awe" in the sense of a "reverence full of wonder and fear" comes closest, though the word "fear" still needs some further exploration. In scripture we encounter two types of fear which, once they are clearly distinguished, can bring us closer to the heart of that religious experience of the *fascinosum et tremendum* (fascinating and awesome).

16. Two Kinds of Fear

There is a fear which Webster defines as "an unpleasant often strange emotion caused by anticipation or awareness of danger." Whenever this emotion is misplaced, the word of God wants to relieve us. Moreover, the Bible also wants to protect us from dangers, and to enable us to cope with the inevitable ones. It is said that the Old Testament tells us 365 times: "Do not be afraid"; one reminder for each day of the year. Let us quote just one of many examples: "Fear not, I am with you; be not dismayed; I am your God" (Is 41:10). In the New Testament both John and Paul immediately come to mind: "There is no fear in love, but perfect love drives out fear" (1 Jn 4:18); "You did not receive a spirit of slavery to fall back into fear, but you received a spirit of adoption, through which we cry, Abba, Father" (Rom 8:15).

Positive Fear

There is also a fear which is highly praised in scripture: as the beginning and the fullness of wisdom, as the source of gladness, joy and length of days (cf. Sir 1:11-20). It is the gate to God's mercy (cf. Jdt 16:15). In fact, it is the only thing which God demands from us: "And now, Israel, what does the Lord your God ask of you but to fear the *Lord*, your God, and follow his ways exactly, to love and serve the *Lord*, your God, with all your heart and all your soul, to keep the commandments and statutes of the *Lord* which I enjoin on you today for your own good?" (Dt 10:12-13). "The last word, when all is heard: Fear God and keep his commandments, for this is our all" (Eccl = Qo 12:13). We could even capture the ten commandments under the one heading of this positive fear or profound awe: respect for God in his incomparability; for the name and the day of the Lord; for parents and life; for marriage and sexuality, for property, right, and truth.

Jesus also rouses this fear time and again which the gospel narrative apparently rates as positive. One example is the occasion when Jesus raised the widow's son at Nain: "Fear seized them all, and they glorified God, exclaiming, 'A great prophet has risen in our midst' and 'God has visited his people' (Lk 7:16).

This second kind of fear is completely different from anxiety. It is wonder and astonishment, breathless amazement. There is a sense of awe for the holiness and splendor of God in it, together with a determined longing to live accordingly. The body language expresses this awe so clearly: taking off one's shoes, a profound bow, paying homage, covering one's face, prostration, and the like. The body, of course, expresses what lives in the mind. One's whole life is at God's service, to keep his commandments is one's heart's desire.

This positive fear implies both distance and familiarity. It is humble reserve as well as loving trust. God is unfathomable mystery and intimate friend. We praise and serve God, but we also bicker, present our complaints, and even our reproaches. Job and Jonah are outstanding examples of this frankness. In many psalms we find prayers in this style, yet always the fear of God is kept alive without which it would no longer be authentic communication with God. In the Talmud we find a profound saying of Rabbi Chanina: "Everything is subjected to the power of heaven, except the fear of God." The Almighty left us free to choose how we would behave toward God, and the decisive element therein is precisely our fear of the Holy One, namely, whether we affirm wholeheartedly the godliness of God. The one thing for which the Almighty depends on us is our free respect and love. Yet, to God, that is the most precious of all. The Most High accepts and loves us as we are; do we accept and love God as God? That is the pinnacle of human freedom. To fathom this freedom ever so slightly is breathtaking. We are free to accept or reject the One who loves us immensely, and to whom we owe our very being. In comparison, all other forms of freedom are but trifles. Rabbi Chanina also suggests that the power of heaven cannot withstand the person who truly fears God.

It is a life-giving paradox that the fear of God liberates us from anxious fear. When we live with a sense of awe for the sovereignty of God, we relativize the adverse powers. Zechariah announced after the birth of his son, John, in a prophetic spirit that God swore "to set us free from the hands of our enemies, free to worship him without fear, holy and righteous in his sight all the days of our life" (Lk 1:74). The ultimate way to overcome anxiety is the fear of God. That might well be its greatest gift.

Only in Hindsight

The book of Exodus recounts a most unusual experience of the *kabod* (Ex 33:12–23). Referring to this passage, a well-known German Old Testament scholar, Fridolin Stier (†1981), wrote in his diary his heartfelt wish:

> To be able, just once, to comment on one of the most grandiose scenes of the Old Testament (Ex 33:17–23), in such a way that after having gone through the usual procedures of scholarship (text, form, tradition, purpose, etc.) at long last the heart of the matter is considered. I mean the desire of a human person, Moses, to see the face, the *kabod* of God. That is to say that the exchange of a dialogue, the promise of protection and guidance, do not satisfy Moses any longer; he desires the full experience, the immediate encounter with the reality of God...His desire is thwarted; he is placed in a cleft and God covers Moses' eyes while the *kabod* passes by. "Then I will remove my hand, so that you may see my back; but my face is not to be seen." That is the apex, the ultimate, the extreme allowed to any theology, any philosophy and any scholarship: the back of God—provided they really desire to see his face.[1]

It is hard for Moses to confront Pharaoh, to free the chosen people from tyranny and to lead them through the desert into the promised land. Every so often Moses finds excuses to shirk this frightening mission. In his plight he receives the promise of God: "I myself will go with you, to give you rest." Then Moses makes this bold request: "Do let me see your glory," so as to verify that God is indeed with him and his people. The text then narrates God's answer:

> I will make all my splendor (*kabod!*) pass before you, and in your presence I will pronounce my name, 'LORD'; I who show favors to whom I will, I who grant mercy to whom I will. But my face you cannot see, for no one sees me and still lives. Here, continued the LORD, is a place near me where you shall station yourself on the rock. When my glory passes I will set you in the hollow of the rock and will cover you with my hand, until I have passed by. Then I will remove my hand so that you may see my back; but my face is not to be seen. (Ex 33:19-23)

This stark passage expresses vividly what everyone experiences who seeks God, whether they can verbalize it or not. It is the yearning for the face of God. We are not satisfied to know God from hearsay. It grieves us that in the divine word and the divine name God hides more than what is revealed. The obscurity of prayer weighs heavily. We long for nothing less than the face of God, for the glory of the Holy One. This longing cannot be fulfilled here on earth; we never see more than the back of God. The undaunted, unquenchable pining for contemplating God with unveiled face is like a constant thorn in the flesh. The deepest human desire is beyond our efforts. The art of the spiritual life is to live with this unquenched thirst without giving up and without settling for substitutes. It is like walking a crest. There is the constant temptation to fill up the gap with possessions and entertainment, activities and relationships, words or thoughts, perhaps even about God.

When the *kabod* passes by, we are in the dark cleft of the rock, covered by God's hand and see absolutely nothing. Only in retrospect do we discover that it was precisely at that time that God was nearest. That is the way life with God is. In the hardest periods of our life's journey, there is only one pair of footprints in the sand; and we wonder where the other pair has gone. In great suffering God seems distant and we feel deserted. Perhaps only years later shall we discover how close God really was and how fruitful this time was. A contemplative once shared with me how a few simple lines provided her an anchor in a time of crisis: "An hour will come, which makes clear to us, that what once confused us, was, in fact, a silent ripening. And, gratefully our heart realizes, that everything, everything is grace." That was the experience of St. Thérèse of Lisieux at the end of her life, when she kept repeating: *tout est grâce*, everything is grace. Søren Kierkegaard is right in his sober remark: "Life is lived forward but understood backward."

17. With the Eyes of Faith

We can see the back of God in creation, if we have learned to look with the eyes of faith, since "heaven and earth are full of your glory (*kabod*)" (cf. Is 6:3). We still sing it in every liturgy. "The heavens proclaim the glory of God and the firmament shows forth the work of his hands" (Ps 19:2). That happens without word or sound; yet the message goes forth to the ends of the earth (v 4–5). "The skies proclaim God's justice; all peoples see his glory" (Ps 97:6). "Yes, the earth shall be filled with the knowledge of God's glory as water covers the sea" (Hab 2:14, cf. Is 11:9).

The Russian pilgrim, who in the middle of the last century applied himself with great fervor to the Jesus-prayer, describes this experience: "When I prayed with my heart, everything around me seemed delightful and marvelous. The trees, the grass, the birds, the earth, the air, the light seemed to be telling me that they existed for our sake, that they witnessed to the love of God for us, that everything proved the love of God for us, that all things prayed to God and sang the praise of the Holy One. Thus it was that I came to understand what the Philokalia calls 'the knowledge of the speech of all creatures.'[1]

It is of vital importance to perceive nature and the whole world this way. If we do not learn to discover the divine *kabod* here on earth, we banish God into the hereafter, thus robbing the world of its heart. We ourselves then eliminate God, doing injustice to God and playing havoc with the earth. We flatten out and banalize creation. It loses its symbolic force, its transparency, its, so to say, sacramental character. It is no longer compre-

114

hended as a radiance of God's *kabod,* as a manifestation of God's self-communication. We efface one of the great blessings of our faith. "We could say that the great mystery of Christianity is not exactly the appearance, but the transparency of God in the universe. In a word, God is to be recognized not in special visions, but in the way divinity shines forth like shook foil through all creation for all with eyes of faith to see."[2]

If we neglect this faith-vision, we create a split between God and the world. We isolate God, as if the Most High were basically unrelated to our world and unaffected by what happens in it. By the same token, we profane the earth, as if ecology, reduction of armaments, help to developing countries, debt of Third World nations, etc., have nothing to do with God. All these things are of the utmost importance for future generations. With none of them can we cope only with political or ethical means. The roots of the solution go deeper. We need a holy reverence for the creation entrusted by the creator to our stewardship, which recognizes in it God's inexhaustible *kabod.* A more pronounced sense for this *kabod* is a very precious and timely gift for the present and the future human family. It can provide the foundation for the desperately needed change in our dealings with all of life and with all of nature. The ecological movement cannot be successful without a profound spirituality to support it.

God's glory can be recognized in nature, then clearly so in the crown of creation, the human person. Classical are the bold words of Bishop Irenaeus of Lyons, France (†202): "The glory of God is the human person fully alive." The other half of the sentence is not always quoted with it: "The life of the human person is the vision of God." And the context is seldom mentioned: "The glory of God provides life. Those contemplating Christ receive a share of life."[3] The life-affirming thoughts of Irenaeus find their basis in the beginning of scripture where "God said, 'Let us make man in our image, after our likeness...God created man in his image, in the divine image he created him; male and female he created them" (Gen 1:26–27). The Eastern Church in her liturgy takes this text very seriously as the faithful pray in fitting self-respect: "I remain an icon of your inexpressible glory even when I am disfigured by sin."

Source of Fulfillment

The *kabod* provides the foundation for the joy of the good news. From God's *kabod* springs the human greatness and from God's mercy the new creation (cf. 2 Cor 5:17). Whoever is touched by the unattainable greatness of God will have respect for the greatness of the human person. A lively faith in God gives rise to a faithful relationship to the earth and especially to our fellow men and women. Those with this respect perceive something more than those without it. They see the mystery at the heart of people and things.

In the small part of his Spiritual Diary which is preserved, St. Ignatius speaks often about strong feelings of respect. The entry of March 14, 1544, reads, "During all these times before, during and after Mass, I had a steady thought which penetrated the depth of my soul. How great is the reverence and affectionate awe with which I ought to pronounce the name of God our Lord, and so on; and further, that I ought to seek not tears, but this affectionate awe and reverence." In the next fourteen days the entries are usually brief; yet each time the affectionate awe is mentioned. On Sunday, March 30, he writes at dawn: "During this period of time I kept on thinking that humility, reverence, and affectionate awe ought to be not fearful but loving. This thought took root in my mind so deeply that I begged over and over again: 'Give me loving humility, and with it reverence and affectionate awe.' ·

In the course of that day this reverence and affectionate awe expanded so as also to include creation: "Later during the day I experienced great joy in remembering this. It seemed to me that I ought not to stop there, but that the same would apply in relation to creatures; that is to say, loving humility and all it brings would so apply."[4] This loving humility becomes a basic attitude for Ignatius, which he also expects from his followers as he expresses several times in the Constitutions; e.g. the novices should "turn their lover upon the Creator of all things, by loving

God in all creatures and all of them in God, in conformity with His holy and divine will."[5]

His confreres portrayed Ignatius as a man of great respect. With this attitude he could envisage creator and creatures in one view. He was contemplative in his action, finding God in everything. This union with God concretized in respect, which is the only attitude that does justice to the mystery encapsuled in all reality. Therefore, only respect encounters things and people as they are. The primary demand of our time is not control, but respect of creation; it has been the command of scripture from the very beginning. "The greatest thing on earth is respect, because it is the heart of love" (Hermann Schell). Respect will tell whether love is genuine or not. Where respect is lacking, despite any appearance to the contrary, love is also lacking.

The Hasidic tradition passes on the stark statement: "Fear without love is an imperfection; love without fear is nothing at all." The great German poet Johann Wolfgang von Goethe (†1832) puts it in a more polished way: "There is one thing which no one enters the world with, which is nevertheless essential for being an all-around human: respect."

In the ancient Rule of St. Benedict (†547) we encounter the close connection between awe for God's majesty and loving respect for one's neighbor, as these astounding sentences illustrate: The porter will help the visitor "with all the gentleness that comes from the fear of God" (66:4). "All humility should be shown in addressing a guest on arrival or departure. By a bow of the head or by a complete prostration of the body, Christ is to be adored because he is indeed welcomed in them" (53:6–7). In fact, the gospel itself teaches us to deal in this way with the least of our sisters and brothers; in them we encounter Jesus (Mt 25:40,45). The mystery of the incarnation extends much further than we are inclined to think.

Shelter and Protection

The *kabod* is depicted as a shattering reality: no one could see it and still survive. Yet this *kabod* is, at the same time, shelter and protection for human life. Anyone who resists the *kabod*, clashes with an overpowering force. But those who confide themselves to the *kabod*, find out that this force is completely at the service of God's faithfulness and love, or more precisely, is completely one with God's fidelity and love. For the faithful remnant of Israel, "God's glory will be shelter and protection over all: shade from the parching heat of day, refuge and cover from storm and rain" (Is 4:6). To the devout exiles, abducted into captivity in Babylon, the prophet Baruch offers consolation by repeatedly referring to the *kabod*:

> Jerusalem, take off your robe of mourning and misery;
>   put on the splendor of glory from God forever.
> Wrapped in the cloak of justice from God,
>   bear on your head the mitre
>   that displays the glory of the eternal name.
> For God will show all the earth your splendor;
>   you will be named by God forever
>   the peace of justice, the glory of God's worship
>
> For God has commanded
>   that every lofty mountain be made low,
> And that the age-old depths and gorges
>   be filled to level ground,
>   that Israel may advance secure in the glory of God.
>   (Bar 5:1–4, 7)

The greatest dangers for humankind are not the exploitation of the earth, the devastation of our life-supporting environment, the threat of nuclear disasters or the manipulation of genes. Surely, these are causes for alarm of a global dimension, which we cannot take seriously enough. Yet they do not touch the ultimate in us. St. Paul speaks about the possibility of losing God's glory. That would ravage the inner recesses of our human existence, upset the deepest ground of our being. It would turn the security, which we find in the divine *kabod*, into its complete opposite. It would be the "no," that stifles true life altogether. The stream, cut off from its source, dries up. That is what happens in sin, if we take Paul's word in its profoundly existential sense. The letter to the Romans states, "All have sinned and are deprived of the glory of God" (3:23). It should be added, however, that Paul makes this statement in that part of his letter which treats of God's completely undeserved mercy and grace. The greatness of our remission corresponds to the depth of the fall.

18. The Wholly Other

It is not pleasant to focus on God's *kabod*. It both elevates and shames us. In the *kabod*, above all, God is the wholly other. Usually the similarities between God and ourselves are more appealing, and they are always more accessible. On the occasion of his eightieth birthday, Karl Rahner, in his hometown of Freiburg, Germany, gave an address which turned out to be his last major discourse.[1] Its title was: "Experiences of a Catholic Theologian." His main theme was one which purposely permeated so many of his writings: the awe and adoration of the incomprehensible and unwieldly mystery of God. It was fitting that this came to be the theme of his swan song.

The first experience he talked about immediately penetrated deeply into the doctrine and the praxis of our faith. He pointed out that somewhere in every theological textbook we always find the explicit remark that our speech about God is invariably analogical, and that in this analogy the dissimilarity between our human words and the divine reality is always greater than the articulated similarity. But usually this vital truth is soon forgotten in our further speaking of God. Every true and valid affirmation about the divine should, in a certain sense, be negated at the same time. Without this eerie hovering between yes and no, our assertions would be too simple and would in fact ignore the mystery of divine reality. It is obvious that the ineffable otherness of God renders all our thinking and speaking about God very cumbersome. We must constantly remain aware of the inappropriateness of our words, and keep expressing this inadequacy, lest the hearer or the speaker forget that God "dwells in unapproachable light" (1 Tim 6:16).

All our words must be dropped into the silent incomprehensibility of God. No need to say that the temptation to have at least a certain limited amount of control can easily entice us. To relate adequately to the divine *kabod* demands of us such a restraint, that few of us persist. How easily we deteriorate into talking or thinking about God as a well-known friend, like a human person, if not like an object! How quickly we speak about the will of God as something we have surely discerned. How many theological and, especially, church-political discussions almost fall off into an ideology, because our ignorance is forgotten or disowned.

We sometimes have the impertinenece to assert or deny something about God's intentions, because "we could not imagine otherwise." What do we think we can "imagine" about God anyway? Are we not forgetting once again that our ideas fall infinitely short of the unfathomable greatness of God? How seldom do our assertions made from university chairs, or pulpits, or in discussions vibrate the diffidence which behooves creatures speaking about the inexpressible. "How seldom comes across that all our utterances about the divine are only the last moment before the blessed muteness that permeates even heaven's clear face-to-face vision of God" (Karl Rahner). Little did Karl Rahner know when he said this how close he was himself to this last moment. Or had he more misgiving than we realize?

There is no doubt a silence and an avoidance of God which is shallow and stems from a lack of religious empathy. This type of silence is, of course, poles apart from the holy reticence of people touched by God's *kabod*. It requires much selfless ascetism to have our image of God corrected all the time. That is a very painful letting-go. The true God need not correspond to our expectations; God always remains unpredictable and often enough staggering. "My thoughts are not your thoughts, nor are your ways my ways, says the Lord. As high as the heavens are above the earth, so high are my ways above your ways and my thoughts above your thoughts" (Is 55:8–9).

Incomprehensible

To let God be God means to accept the divine mystery, and therefore to live in wonder and suspense. It implies giving up control. It is certain that God is love, that God loves us into existence, that the Most High accepts us unconditionally as we are and wants our lives to come to a rich unfolding and abundant fruitfulness. However, we do not know in advance what this means concretely and how God gives shape to this immense love; we only find it out in retrospect. The mystery which God is, is full of surprises and only those who open up to the Holy One with truly open hands and open heart can live faith-fully.

God's mysteriousness is not lessened in the incarnation of the word, but rather brought to a more intense pitch. Jesus in no way dispenses us from this radical openness. He demands from his followers an unconditional willingness to put their entire future at stake for the kingdom. "Foxes have dens and birds of the sky have nests, but the Son of Man has nowhere to rest his head," is his answer to someone who wants to follow him wherever he goes (Lk 9:58). Den and nest are obvious symbols of security and comfort for which the human heart naturally craves. Jesus has renounced them; he wants his disciples to do the same. The only home of Jesus is his Abba and the will of his Abba. For the reign of God and its *kabod* we, too, have to abandon everything. Precisely in this radical summons, Jesus reveals himself as the one who knows the Most High (cf. Lk 10:22), and who in his complete intimacy with his Abba always cherishes the divine *kabod*.

The gifted German sculptor, Ernst Barlach (†1938), who suffered much distress, once said: "I have no God." Someone might understand from that remark that he was an atheist. The next sentence clears up this misunderstanding. "I praise him for being who he is. I have no God, but God has me." That faith gave him the strength he needed in his trials.

The exegete Fridolin Stier, whom we quoted previously in chapter 16, once captured this fantasy in his diary:

When the cardinal inquisitor asked me whether I believed in God, I answered: "No, I do not believe in your God." When the atheist asked me whether I believed in God, I responded again: "No, I do not believe in the God whom you deny." If I had given an affirmative answer to the questions of the cardinal and the atheist, I would have been dishonest with both of them. I would have deceived them recklessly. Each would have identified *the* God in whom I declared to believe, with his—confessed or denied—God. "So you do believe in a God" the cardinal and the atheist retorted with one voice. "In GOD, please, not in *a* god, as you do. Not in *a* nor in *mine*, not in *this* neither in *that* because they are all gods. GOD is at odds with these gods and with us, who honor or destroy their images; and so God is the most militant atheist. The inquisitor condemned me as a blasphemer; the atheist scorned and demeaned me as quite a character.[2]

This helps us to understand Meister Eckhart when he says: "I pray God to liberate me from God."

Do Not Utilize God

In this decalogue God forbids us to take his name in vain (Ex 20:7). This seems to imply: "You shall not let me say what suits you." We are not supposed to use God and religion to support our own interests, no matter how devout they may seem. God is not the offspring of our desires and needs. God does not exist for the world, but the world, and especially humankind, exists for God. Let us refer once again to the unambiguous opening sentence of the Spiritual Exercises: "Human beings are created to praise, reverence, and serve God, and by means of doing this to save their souls" (23). There is no doubt that to serve God is the best way to unfold our personality both in this world and in the next. This, though, does not turn God into an instrument for our self-realization. On the contrary, the human self-realization on earth and in heaven is a fruit of our surrender to God. We could compare it with friendship, which usually yields certain fringe benefits. Yet whoever attempts a friendship because of these advantages, does not reach a genuine friendship at all, but rather degrades and drains it. Such a person perverts a precious gift into a platitude, and in doing so harms one's self greatly.

Simarly (though the comparison limps) it would be a corruption of faith to claim the divine *kabod* for our advantage no matter how sublime this may be. God can in no way be used, and genuine faith has always been aware of this. We must not degrade God to a (cheap or costly) answer to our (real or imaginary) questions. God is beyond that and always remains a huge question and challenge to us. God's majesty is not at our beck and call. Someone who thinks and lives in that way reduces God to human proportions and inflates the human person to ultimate importance, an "honor" too heavy for our shoulders. In doing so we have intrinsically blocked the road to happiness and fulfillment.

The cross, which everyone encounters in the reality of daily life, unmasks this unreal self-glorification. The cross is ever foolishness and a stumbling block; we can never comprehend it. The attempt to have everything under control to the point of incorporating the divine mystery (and in so doing denying its mysteriousness) certainly fails once the cross enters into our life. Conversely, on the cross the authenticity of Jesus' relationship with his Abba was manifested.[3] Thus, each of us will time and again experience the *kabod* as a cross, which scruitinizes the genuineness of our relationship with God. After all, divine majesty and human dignity are, notwithstanding all similarity, radically dissimilar. That hurts.

Religious practices and achievements can degenerate into a seemingly devout attempt to force the entrance into the mystery of God; in other words, to make God available. As soon as we try to have a grip on God, we become tense and anxious. This is the danger of legalism which does not come to fulfillment in love (cf. Mt 5:17). Such legalism shields us from the unpredictable surprises of God. In the endeavor to restrain God, we close ourselves off from the infinite greatness. The Pharisee as we encounter him in the gospel, is the prototype of the person who succumbed to this temptation. Still, the prophet Zechariah had already warned against this constriction, which in fact results from little faith. In his third vision he proclaims:

I raised my eyes and looked; there was a man with a measuring line in his hand. "Where are you going?" I asked. "To measure Jerusalem," he answered; "to see how great is its width and how great its length."

Then the angel who spoke with me advanced, and another angel came out to meet him, and said to him, "Run, tell this to that young man: People will live in Jerusalem as though in open country, because of the multitude of men and beasts in their midst. But I will be for her an encircling wall of fire, says the Lord, and I will be the glory in her midst" (Zec 2:5–9).

As in many prophecies, Jerusalem is an image of the church. She is not to be exclusive, but inclusive. Scripture has especially in mind a wholehearted welcome to the poor, the widows and the orphans, the victims of injustice and oppression. God's place is always at their side, and the Most High will be the glory in the midst of Jerusalem and the church, when they take these poor to heart in a special way.

19. The Ineffable Name

At the burning bush God entrusted to Moses the mission to lead the chosen people from slavery into freedom. God reveals his name: JHWH, as support and guarantee in this difficult venture. But it is a revelation which after thousands of years still has not given away its secret and never will. The usual translation is, "I am who am" or "I am who I am." The name remains open; it does not define God. It is not static, but unfolds itself continuously. It does not give a circumscription of God's essence, but denotes a dynamic presence. The content of the name remains mysterious; no "who" or "where" or "when" is revealed. Yet the existential conveyance of the name is enormous: it communicates the unlimited active presence, the absolute reliability. Moses can depend on this name in his mission, as can each of us.

The numinous name JHWH keeps in balance the nearness and the distance in our relationship to God. God is at the same time transcendent—that means infinitely beyond all earthly and human reality; and immanent—which means that he is living in all that is as its innermost mystery, its Deepest Ground. The immanence is God's intimate indwelling which pervades and quickens our world; the transcendence surpasses any confinement in this world. The two may seem opposites to us, but are in fact correlative aspects of the Ineffable. Disregard of God's immanence banishes God far away from our lives, and turns the Holy One into a distant outsider with whom we have hardly any relationship; it is like ostracizing God. In the extreme it renders the world and humankind godless. This obviously entails an enormous loss of meaningfulness and of genuine fulfillment in our life. On the other hand, inattention to God's transcendence robs God of greatness and power, reducing the Most High to someone who fits into this world. The extreme case would have God and the world equal each other; the world would have become God; fatalism and apathy would take over.

Experience is proving more and more convincingly that a world deprived of its Deepest Ground cannot be soundly sustained. When the world becomes an idol, humankind blatantly exploits creation so frantically that it starts to destroy precisely that which it claims to be the ultimate. The deification of the world stifles her. As the ecological movement grows, this fact is dawning now on an increasing number of people. The reaction to this exploitation is important, yet very precarious. If we remain on the same level of equalizing God and the world, the awareness of environmental misuse may go to the other extreme: an over-cautiousness, which once again boarders on idolization, but now from the other side. A remarkable phenomenon is that this over-cautiousness occasionally has blind spots. It can be quite inconsistent. Could this indicate a lack of depth?

St. Augustine in his *Confessiones* (111, 6,11) summarized, in words which have become classic, the synthesis of transcendence and immanence as our faith perceives it: "God is more intimate than my deepest self and higher than my utmost peak." The Holy One is nearer and more faithful to me than I am myself. The Most High loves me more, much more, than I could possibly love myself. God is more immanent in me than I am myself. Precisely that surplus of immanence is the divine transcendence. The latter is not some kind of insensitivity to human suffering or joy, but an indwelling and intimacy which surpasses our human measure.

God, the rock of faithfulness and reliability, who carries us no matter what, is not to be confused with anything or anyone, but everything and everyone is to be understood in relation to the Most High. God is the one, without whom nothing is (Peter Knauer).

Holiness

Scripture closely connects the immanent-transcendent *kabod* with God's holiness. Glory and holiness are both jealously reserved for the Most High. They correspond to God's inner-most self. *Kabod* and holiness cannot be understood from cre-ation only; they have to be revealed to us. Their origin is unambiguously in God alone. They belong to the unfathomable mystery, which we call God. "Who can stand in the presence of this Holy One?" the inhabitants of Beth-Shemesh asked anxious-ly when the ark of the covenant, the great sign of God's presence among his people, had been brought from the land of the Philistines into their town (1 Sam 6:20). God's *kabod* and holi-ness are unbearable for human beings. They summon us: "Be holy, for I, the Lord, your God, am holy" (Lev 19:2); in fact, it is God who makes us holy: "...I, the Lord, who make you holy..." (Lev 20:8). God is the fountain of all holiness, as the second eucharist prayer says. The Most High alone can forgive sins (cf. Mk 2:7); without this forgiveness there is no access to holiness.

Again, like the *kabod*, so also holiness breaks into our human realm in the strength of its own dynamics. One form is the offer of forgiveness of our sins, but before that, comes the disclosure of our guilt. As long as we restrict our view to focusing on our-selves, we can to some extent fool ourselves. The holiness of the Wholly Other unmasks all illusions and self-righteousness. It probes heart and soul. The God, whom Jesus calls Abba and to whom he leads us, is not an easygoing grandparent, nor a deity according to our liking. In all his unconditional love and mercy, this Abba is also the all-holy and just judge.

In the vision recorded in the first chapter of the book of Revelation (v 12–18), the Chosen One appears between seven golden lampstands with eyes like fiery flames and a sharp dou-ble-edged sword coming out of his mouth. In the letter to the Hebrews it is said still more clearly: "The Word of God is living and effective, sharper than any two-edged sword, penetrating even between soul and spirit, joints and marrow, and able to dis-cern reflections and thoughts of the heart. No creature is concealed from him, but everything is naked and exposed to the eyes of him to whom we must render an account" (4:12–13). God, whom we have tamed in our habits, fettered to our convenience, neutralized in our mediocrity, made manageable by our consumerism, yet sees through our rationalizations, unmasks our repressions and judges our intentions. The splendor of God's holiness makes our whole self transparent. That is the judgment. It need not be verbalized at all; in this clarity it is self-evident. It is absolute truth.

One who has a sense of this holiness will often pray with inner conviction, as Ignatius advises the retreatant to do at the beginning of each prayer period: "To ask God our Lord for the grace that all my intentions, actions, and operations may be ordered purely to the service and praise of the Divine Majesty" (Sp Ex 46). It is a prayer which corresponds to the Principle and Foundation (Sp Ex 23) and is articulated in the form of a petition. Also, it is a prayer teeming with tremendous dynamics, since serving and praising God implies a call to spread the divine glory. The latter encompasses the whole world and all of humankind. This must be revealed through our actions. The faithfully-repeated preparatory prayer deepens this disposition and enhances an apostolic, missionary spirit.

Mission

In the Bible the encounter with the *kabod* transforms a person into an apostle. We mentioned at the beginning of chapter 15 the vision of Isaiah, which concludes with the verse: "Then I heard the voice of the Lord saying, 'Whom shall I send? Who will go for us?' 'Here I am.' I said: 'send me!" (6:8). Likewise, Peter is sent after the awesome experience of the miraculous catch of fish, which brought home to him so forcefully Jesus' transcendence: "Do not be afraid; from now on you will be catching men" (Lk 5:10). Such a profound encounter is never intended just for the one person privileged with it. It is given to one person in order to be fruitful for many. On the other hand, without some experience of the *kabod* no one can be an apostle;

one could only preach a mini-god. Such people would build far too much on their own strength and preach too much their own self. To have brushed the *kabod* is the foundation of genuine apostolic mission.

That is why humility is so vital for the apostle. St. Paul writes: "As I see it, God has exhibited us apostles as the last of all..." (1 Cor 4:9).

To accept this is a challenge which requires lifelong wrestling with ourselves. Just to understand what the concept of humility means is hard enough. It is so often misunderstood. In this frequent misconception a certain subconscious resistance to humility might well play a role.

20. Humility

Obviously humility is not to be equated with inferiority feelings, a poor self-image, or diffidence. These, rather, seem to indicate a lack of humility. Humility is more than an awareness and an admission of one's weaknesses. It is often said that humility is truth; this saying refers to the fact that there is no perfect spouse, no perfect parent, no perfect daughter or son; no perfect community, no perfect superior or leader or CEO, no perfect church and no perfect state. We ourselves are not perfect either, nor are our deeds. To accept this state of affairs requires courage. Only then can something change for the better, since we can only transform what we have accepted. This is all very true; yet humility is more than that.

In the last analysis, humility means to focus more on God or Jesus than on self.[1] Orientation toward God's glory is decisive. A genuinely humble person is fascinated by God's beauty and holiness, and is thereby released from complexity and complexes in daily life. Humility means to sense the abyss which separates God and us, and at the same time (without ignoring this abyss), the love that unites us. Humility, then is closely related to adoration which is the heartfelt desire that God be God. Because God is God, the human person can be human. Humility is the basic attitude that corresponds to this intrinsic structure of all reality. Humility does not hold on to self, neither to one's success nor to one's frustrations, neither to one's joy nor to one's grief. That is why true humility is never discouraged. It is a source of trust, of courage, and above all of supple, indefatigable perseverance. This perseverance is poles apart from stubbornness, obstinacy, rigidity, fanaticism or blazing enthusiasm. It is characterized by peace and faithfulness. Its hallmarks are confidence and abandonment. Pride, and pride alone, is susceptible to discouragement. Humility is also ready to accept suffering, if that is part of the mission. Where this readiness is lacking, bitterness lies in wait. Discouragement and bitterness are the antithesis of humility.

Not to Make Comparisons

Chesterton is insightful when he considers humor as the natural foundation for humility. Even more to the point is Dag Hammarskjöld's terse statement: "Humility is just as much the opposite of self-abasement as it is of self-exaltation. To be humble is *not to make comparisons*."[2] Comparing is in reality a circling around self. It turns the other person into a satellite of the ego and, most important of all, loses God from sight. Humble people are never rivals. They do not engage in competitiveness, which is obviously based entirely on constant comparison. They are peacemakers, not because they water down the contrasts, or try at all costs to comply, but because they live in harmony with God and draw their authentic feelings of self-worth from their Abba. This brings forth Shalom, for themselves and through them for others.

In the parable that Jesus addressed "to those who were convinced of their own righteousness and despised everyone else" (Lk 18:9–14), the Pharisee compares himself with the publican. In this comparison he stands out as the better person (at least in his own eyes). But even if in the comparison the Pharisee had considered himself as the lesser one, it would still not have been humility. The tax collector does not compare at all; he concentrates simply on God, to whom he would not even raise his eyes. That is humility.

Teresa of Avila warns without any ifs, ands, or buts: comparing is the death of the spiritual life. It introduces false standards, which divert and confuse, and in the long run, suffocate.

Humility has nothing in common with cowardice or human respect, with anxiousness or insecurity; much less with obstinacy or callousness. On the contrary, true humility liberates us from unhealthy dependence and releases us from the fear of public opinion, while simultaneously conveying a genuine sensitivity and courage, precisely because it looks at God and senses his *kabod*. Remember St. Benedict's rule: "With all the gentleness that comes from the fear of God" (66:4). From there it draws the courage to follow the road, which it recognizes in God's light as the correct one.

Lack of humility has done so much harm in families, in communities, in ministries. From lack of humility, some are people-pleasers and others are careerists. During all of the public life of Jesus, every so often we encounter among the disciples sad examples of both kinds of weaknesses. During the trial and mockery of Jesus, Peter yields to human respect and says to the people around the charcoal fire: "I do not know him" (Lk 22:57). After the third prediction of the passion the sons of Zebedee succumb to careerism and approach Jesus with the callous request for the first places in the kingdom to come. The Acts of the Apostles record many of these weaknesses; in fact, in the whole history of Christianity they never disappear. That is one of those things one could good-naturedly say, and there is a certain wisdom in this approach. Scripture teaches us more profoundly that God works despite, and even in, our failures; that is the way God's creativity continues. There is yet a greater wisdom in this view. But, notwithstanding all this wisdom, lack of humility does harm to the credibility of the church and causes much unnecessary human suffering, if not downright injustice. The more we open ourselves for God's *kabod*, the more the reign of God is realized in this world. There is no doubt that this is the attitude to which Jesus calls us and in which he himself lived.

An old Franciscan summed up eloquently how bringing our burden to God and concentrating on him instead of on self, opens a completely new life. The text conveys beautifully what humility is all about.

I heard an aged confrere, wise and good, perfect and holy, say: if you feel the call of the Spirit, then be holy with all your soul, with all your heart, and with all your strength.

If, however, because of human weakness you cannot be holy, then be perfect with all your soul, with all your heart, and with all your strength.

But, if you cannot be perfect because of vanity in your life, then be good with all your soul, with all your heart, and with all your strength.

Yet, if you cannot be good because of the trickery of the Evil One, then be wise with all your soul, with all your heart, and with all your strength.

If, in the end, you can be neither holy, nor perfect, nor good, nor wise because of the weight of your sins, then carry this weight before God and surrender your life to His divine mercy.

If you do this, without bitterness, with all humility, and with a joyous spirit due to the tenderness of a God who loves the sinful and ungrateful, then you will begin to feel what it is to be wise, you will learn what it is to be good, you will slowly aspire to be perfect, and finally you will long to be holy.

If you do all this, with all your soul, with all your heart, and with all your strength, then I assure you, my brother, you will be on the path of Saint Francis, you will not be far from the Kingdom of God.[3]

We Saw His Glory

The message of the Old Testament is intensified and fulfilled in the New Testament. A prime element of this shift is that in Jesus the *kabod* becomes visible. The inaccessible glory of God is revealed in Jesus and shows itself in him to be most attractive. One example is how the mysterious Servant of Yahweh in the four songs of Deutero-Isaiah, is in the New Testament repeatedly identified with Jesus: "You are my servant Israel, through whom I show my glory" (Is 49:3). The transference is striking in John's gospel; after having quoted two texts from Isaiah, the evangelist interprets: "Isaiah said this because he saw his glory and spoke about him" (Jn 12:41). Now, Isaiah saw the glory of *Yahweh* enthroned in the heavenly temple but John refers it directly to *Jesus* and really says: "Isaiah saw Jesus' glory and spoke about Jesus." Similarly, Paul, in his second letter to the Corinthians argues in a polemic with his former colleagues, the Pharisees, that only in Christ is the veil, which lies over Moses (i.e., the Old Testament), removed (3:12–18). Christian liturgy constantly uses this interpretation of scripture; so the psalm verse "O gates, lift high your heads; grow higher, ancient doors. Let him enter, the king of glory" (24:7,9) is applied to Jesus on several feasts. Also, the verse which originally referred to the manna, is sung with a slight change on Christmas eve: "Today you will know that the Lord is coming to save us, and in the morning you will see his glory" (Ex 16:6–7).

When Jesus was born the glory of the Lord shone around the shepherds (Lk 2:9) and a multitude of the heavenly host sang the name (i.e., the identity) of the new-born: "Glory to God in the highest and on earth peace to those on whom his favor rests" (Lk 2:14). "Jesus is the refulgence of God's glory, the very imprint of God's being" (Heb 1:3). Jesus is "the image of the invisible God" (Col 1:15). The entire earthly life of Jesus is a veiled epiphany: just as the *kabod* of Yahweh had its abode among the people of Israel in the tent of the covenant under the cloud, so the glory of God has pitched its tent among us in the person of Jesus, from whose fullness we all receive grace upon grace. "No one has ever seen God. The only Son, God, who is at the Father's side, has revealed him" (Jn 1:18). In signs and miracles Jesus discloses every so often a little bit more of the fullness of his glory. The signs are meant to lead us to faith, but on the other hand for complete understanding, they also presuppose faith: "If you believe, you will see the glory of God" (Jn 11:40).

To Touch Jesus

In the oldest gospel passed on to us, Mark describes how Jesus reacted to being touched: "Jesus asked, 'Who has touched me?' But his disciples said to him, 'You see how the crowd is pressing upon you, and yet you ask, 'Who touched me?' And he looked around to see who had done it" (5:30–32). Apparently there is a noncommittal, sterile contact with Jesus, as many people in the crowd had; but there is also conscious, healing contact, which the woman afflicted with hemorrhages for twelve years, sought and found. The Holy One can be physically contacted. The Inaccessible has come close. From now on it depends on us how genuine and beneficial this touch is.

Also, people who did not recognize him have touched him. Some of them "have crucified the Lord of glory" (1 Cor 2:8). Precisely this crucifixion is interpreted in the New Testament, especially in John, as Jesus' glorification because it makes manifest his love to the very end. It is this love that lets him lay down his life for his friends (Jn 13:1; 15:13). The love to the end is a self-emptying leading to the death on a cross. That is the glorification as God understands it. It is not a career that competes for the first place, for being faster, smarter, bigger, better, more efficient, and more successful than others, but a downward career, which accepts deliberately the lowest place. Whenever Jesus speaks about his glorification, he means his shame, his failure, his death on the cross. "Was it not necessary that the Messiah should suffer these things and so enter into his glory?" (Lk 24:26). God "has glorified his servant Jesus whom you handed over and rejected...(Acts 3:13).

We are privileged to share in this glory: "God calls us into his kingdom and glory" (1 Thes 2:12). "To this end God has called us through our gospel to possess the glory of Our Lord Jesus" (2 Thes 2:14). "The God of all grace called us to his eternal glory through Christ Jesus..." (1 Pt 5:10). According to the beautiful text of Second Corinthians it is through contemplating the very glory of God, as incarnated in Jesus, that we are transformed into his image (icon). This becomes all the more significant when we remember that the letter to the Romans pinpoints the meaning and end of our lives precisely in our being conformed to the image of Jesus (8:29). "We with our unveiled faces reflecting like mirrors the glory of the Lord, all grow brighter and brighter as we are turned into the image that we reflect; this is the work of the Lord who is spirit" (2 Cor 3:18 JB).

That means also for us a downward career, inasmuch as that corresponds to the image and glory of Jesus. Since the Roman Synod of Bishops of 1971, it has become commonplace that faith necessarily implies the promotion of justice, and that justice in the Bible includes a special care for the poor, oppressed, helpless, and handicapped. Jesus indeed lived deliberately in solidarity with the poor and the weak. In this he is the true image of God, whom he calls his Abba, and who all through the Old Testament took the side of the victims of injustice. A constant theme that runs through all of the Old and New Testament becomes visible. Who searches for the glory of God, can find it only on the road to and with the poor. In them God reveals his *kabod*, most clearly in his son, who became one of them.

VI

THE PASCHAL MYSTERY

21. The Passion in the Light of the Resurrection

✪

More than a century ago the German exegete Martin Kähler launched the provocative paradox that the gospel of Mark is the story of the passion with an elaborate introduction. If we remember that gospel means "good news," we certainly have a paradox here. So the "glad tidings" is basically the account of the unjust, brutal, and lethal suffering of an innocent man! That is really stretching it a little far!

Yet, Kähler in his deliberate overstatement has a point. He considers the passion to be the heart of Mark's gospel; the other chapters only lead up to it. First, there are the thirty years of Jesus' hidden life, which are not mentioned at all in Mark, and dealt with in just a couple of pages in Matthew and Luke. The public life of Jesus, then, is related more extensively and in greater detail. But when the passion begins, the pace of the narrative again slows down considerably. All four gospels give us an hour-by-hour account. Here we have clearly reached the chief interest of the evangelists.

Kähler's remark is confirmed conspicuously in our official professions of faith, in which the person of Jesus literally has the central place. But between Jesus' birth and his passion nothing seems worth mentioning—not his parables or miracles, his discourses or discussions, his encounters with people or his ministry. From his nativity we skip immediately to his suffering and death. Evidently that constitutes the heart of our faith. The Nicene

141

Creed professes about Jesus: "By the power of the Holy Spirit he was born of the Virgin Mary, and became man. For our sake he was crucified under Pontius Pilate; he suffered, died, and was buried." In the Apostles Creed the omission, proportionally, is even more marked. We say about Jesus: "He was conceived by the power of the Holy Spirit and born of the Virgin Mary. He suffered under Pontius Pilate, was crucified, died, and was buried. He descended to the dead." In the mysteries of the rosary we find the same pattern. They pass from the joyful to the sorrowful mysteries without lingering at all on what happened in between!

In the New Testament there are many texts which emphasize that the passion of Jesus forms the center of our faith in him. It is the ultimate of God's self-giving and self-revelation. St. Paul writes: "God did not spare his own Son but handed him over for us all, how will he not also give us everything else along with him?" (Rom 8:32).

In John's gospel we find a powerful text in which Jesus says to the Jews: "When you lift up the Son of Man, then you will realize that I AM..." (8:28). Jesus claims the most holy Name for himself. This was an unheard of assertion in a milieu where this Name must not be pronounced by human lips. Jesus links his claim with his death on the cross: precisely there his oneness with Yahweh will become manifest. This one verse encompasses the deepest self-emptying—dying like a slave on the cross—and the loftiest self-understanding—equating himself with Yahweh.

Yet no matter how much truth there is in Kähler's paradox, modern exegesis stringently demands an essential expansion. We still can say that the gospel is basically the story of the passion, but of necessity must add that this is seen in the light of the resurrection. Among the many contributions of recent biblical scholarship, the most important one seems to be the evidence that every single page of the gospel is written with the certainty of Jesus' resurrection. It is precisely this all-pervading basic conviction that turns these stories into "good news."

A few examples may help clarify this important insight. The Pharisees could have related the passion of Jesus in much more detail than the evangelists described. After all, they planned to eliminate Jesus and even hired a traitor for this purpose. They executed their plan carefully and relished their success, so they could have undoubtedly reported much that we don't know about. Yet, regardless of how accurate, extensive, and enlightening their presentation would be, it would never be gospel, because faith in the resurrection would be lacking, and so everything would be recounted in a wrong perspective.

One could approach the passion of Jesus as a noble humanist and be very upset by this blatant violation of human rights—perhaps even report it to Amnesty International. But if faith in the resurrection is missing, then we are not dealing with the gospel.

While the disciples were actually present at various stages of the passion, in no way did they experience it as gospel. On the contrary, they felt only a deep disappointment. Their last hope was shattered. They did not expect the resurrection, hence, did not perceive any good news.

The Roman centurion who was in charge of the crucifixion came closest to a true sense of the gospel. Pilate had chosen him for the delicate mission of carrying out the execution of this highly controversial rabbi from Nazareth. Jerusalem was jammed with pilgrims for the Pasch and the condemnation of Jesus could very well be the spark that in this tense atmosphere caused the gunpowder to explode. Pilate made it clear to his trusted officer that he did not want any riots. The centurion on horseback had the whole operation under control and carried it out without a hitch. When the mission was accomplished, this man in charge who had not missed one detail of it, proclaimed: "Truly, this man was the Son of God" (Mk 15:39). We could paraphrase: "In my entire career in the army I have never come across such a crucifixion. This man was extraordinary! I sense genuine holiness in him. He was close to God." The Roman officer had seen in the crucifixion a glimmer of the Beyond. He certainly did not profess a full-fledged Christian faith, nor did his phrase "Son of God" have the full meaning which theology will subsequently and gradually disclose. Nevertheless, he discovered in this suffering man something that transcended the ordinary.

A Christian is a person who sees the horror of the crucifixion in the shining light of the resurrection. When the evangelists wrote their gospels, they saw *more* than they saw during the actual passion, and this "more" constitutes the biblical inspiration. The root of this last work is spirit. The Holy Spirit made them see all that had occurred in the faith of the resurrection. That certainty gave them a new perception. When the early church began reading the historical events of the life of Jesus in the light of the risen Lord, their eyes were opened in many startling discoveries. That is the way the gospels developed. It is the charism of the evangelists, and through them of every Christian, to point out the glistening of the Easter light in the suffering of Jesus— and of his followers. John's gospel especially presents the passion in such a way that the glory of the risen Jesus permeates everything —and occasionally, flashes brightly.

The resurrection is the other face of the passion. It is in a certain sense a dialectical reversal, in which terrible suffering turns into and is fulfilled by enormous joy and glory. But there is above all a continuity between the passion and the resurrection. That is what the inspired texts try to point out to us. The continuity lies in the glory of the love between Father and Son. That love was the sustaining force during the cruel hours of physical and mental suffering. In the resurrection that same love is radiantly revealed. The resurrection is the open manifestation of what was previously the hidden support. The resurrection does not bring the cross to naught, but rather to its ultimate disclosure. Perhaps we could say that in the passion the fidelity of the Son to the Father comes more to the fore, whereas in the resurrection the faithfulness of the Father to his Son is more apparent. Yet in saying so, let us never forget that the two are one; nor let us forget that the love of Father, Son and Holy Spirit to each other is one with the love of the triune God to the world.

In the death on the cross it might look as if the Father had deserted his Son: "My God, my God, why have your forsaken me" (Mk 15:34, Ps 22:1). But the resurrection makes clear that the Father stood by his Son with a fidelity which surpasses our human possibilities and our boldest imagination—in death and beyond death. The resurrection is the uncovering of the eternal and steady love between Father and Son which will be consummated in the outpouring of their common Holy Spirit into our hearts (cf. Rom 5:5): the completion of the paschal mystery.

The paschal mystery consists in the indissoluble unity of the death and the resurrection of Jesus and constitutes the heart of our Christian faith. Death and resurrection are like two sides of a tunnel. A tunnel always has two sides: if it only had one side, it would be just a hole in the ground. And the two sides must be connected; otherwise, there would just be two holes (as was the case in Ufredal, Norway in 1990, where two teams building a mile-and-a-half long tunnel, because of an engineering error did not meet halfway). On the passion side we already catch some glimpses of the Easter light; on the resurrection side we always see the silhouette of the cross through the tunnel just as the risen Lord forever wears the nailmarks in his glorified body. In this way, and in this way only, the paschal mystery is consoling. "Indeed, Jesus was crucified out of weakness, but he lives by the power of God. So also we are weak in him, but...we shall live with him by the power of God" (2 Cor 13:4). "All I want is to know Christ and the power of his resurrection and to share his sufferings..." (Phil 3:10, JB).

It was to this paschal mystery that Jesus referred when he said: "When you lift up the Son of Man, then you will realize that I AM..." (Jn 8:28). A striking confirmation of this powerful verse is that two extremely intelligent Jewish women in the twentieth century came to the Catholic faith precisely through the mystery of the cross. One is Blessed Edith Stein (†1942) who, as a student in Göttingen, Germany, considered herself an atheist until her much appreciated professor Adolf Reinach fell in 1917 on the Belgian front in World War I. The condolence visit with his widow became a turning point in her life. "It was my first encounter with the cross and with the divine strength it conveys to those who carry it. It was the moment in which my unbelief collapsed and Christ radiated: Christ in the mystery of the cross."[1] This was not just a momentary experience. It shaped the rest of her life so much so that as a Carmelite she chose as her name: Sister Teresa Benedicta a Cruce, i.e., Sister Teresa Blessed by the Cross.

The other woman is Simone Weil (†1943). She identified in an extraordinary degree with the suffering of the victims of the Spanish Civil War and of World War II, especially of her fellow Jews under the Nazi terror. She also was struck by the profound connection, which she was graced to perceive, between the god-forsaken situation of these people and of Jesus on the cross. That brought her to the Christian faith. Until a few days before her death, she refused baptism out of a sense of solidarity with her own tormented people. Shortly before she died, she asked a good friend to baptize her.[2] Thus she shared sacramentally in the death and resurrection of Jesus.

Living the Paschal Mystery

The paschal mystery is a dogmatic truth of the highest importance. If Jesus were not risen, we would not have been redeemed. The Easter liturgy does not tire of proclaiming that the same Jesus who hung upon the cross is the one risen from the tomb. To separate the cross and the resurrection is to destroy the central mystery of our faith.

The paschal mystery is also of the utmost practical significance. Whoever believes in this mystery, lives differently. Daily life is transformed. We learn not to waste suffering, for it can bear much fruit if we see the connection with the passion of Jesus. It is very significant that in many of our languages suffering is commonly called "cross." The experience of many generations thus expresses an affinity between our pain and the pain of Jesus. Jesus does not offer us a way out of the disappointments of life, nor does he offer us an explanation which would enable us to understand the meaning of them. He does, however, come to fill our sufferings with his presence. He does not leave us alone in our misery, but he joins us, he who experienced such deep grief himself. He shows us that our distress can be united with his, and thus flow with his passion into the glory of the resurrection. What we spontaneously consider meaningless—and rightly so, because in itself it is—can become creative through the paschal mystery. It guards us from self-pity and bitterness. It makes a tremendous difference.

Suffering, which we are unable to accept with our heart and to integrate into our life, works out negatively. This suffering can have many faces: problems with our health, addictions, setbacks in our career, fair or unfair humiliations, betrayal by those from whom we least expect it, continuous lack of affirmation and recognition, frustrations due to insufficient education, our own immaturities and shadows which we gradually discover, our spiritual mediocrity, long dryness in prayer, our own infidelity, genuine or also inauthentic guilt, and so on. At crucial moments any of these unaccepted sufferings can easily lead us to shallow compensations or to unfaithfulness in our most precious commitments. An unforgiven or perhaps repressed hurt tempts us to hurt others in turn; perhaps we are not even aware of the process that is going on. Our disowned negative experiences bind us in a vicious circle, which results in even more negativism. This can happen in marriage, in religious life, in the priesthood, in single life. It stifles our love, hollows our generosity and ministry, affects our fidelity and honesty, traps us in pettiness and shallowness. The cross of Jesus, perceived in unity with the resurrection, provides a great strength to accept the inevitable, to unite it with the suffering of Jesus, and to render it fruitful.

If we really live our faith in the paschal mystery with integrity we will find consolation not only for ourselves, but also for others. Christian faith is always apostolic. The comfort we offer others must be genuine, deep comfort, rooted in the mystery. A German philosopher chose as the title for one of his books "Only the Mystery Comforts" (Karl Pfleger)[3]. That is the way St. Paul thinks, too: "Blessed be the God and Father of our Lord Jesus Christ, the Father of compassion and God of all encouragement, who encourages us in our every affliction, so that we may be able to encourage those who are in any affliction with the encouragement with which we ourselves are encouraged by God." (2 Cor 1:3–4).

22. Traces of the Glory in the Passion

The bonding of the two sides of the paschal mystery is most advanced in John's gospel. The eagle among the evangelists brooded longer over this mystery than the other three. Whereas the synoptics present the transfiguration at Tabor and the agony in Gethsemane as two distinct occurrences, the fourth gospel lets the two experiences merge (Jn 12:20–33). We read there: "I am troubled now. Yet what should I say? 'Father, save me from this hour?' But it was for this purpose that I came to this hour. Father, glorify your name." These words remind us of the agony in the garden which, apart from these allusions, we do not find in John's gospel. In the same passage we also read: "The hour has come for the Son of Man to be glorified.... A voice came from heaven, 'I have glorified my name and will glorify it again.' The crown heard it and said it was thunder; but others said, 'An angel has spoken to him.'" In these sentences we recognize some slight similarities with the transfiguration, which again is not mentioned in the fourth gospel.

So in John the two episodes, which in the first three gospels refer most clearly to death and glorification, are already assembled into one powerful experience.

The passage begins with the request of some Greeks: "We would like to see Jesus," and ends with Jesus' statement: "When I am lifted up from the earth, I will draw everyone to myself." In this closing verse the crucifixion (John leaves no doubt about the meaning of the words "lifted up from the earth") is pictured as a glorious apotheosis. Indeed, the crucified Lord has drawn numerous people to himself. They have recognized in this man dying on the cross their savior; they have sensed his love and in response feel drawn to him. That is unquestionably the glory of the cross. This closing verse is also the answer to the request of the Greeks to "see" Jesus—they will see him when he is lifted up from the earth. They will have to wait seven chapters to have their petition fulfilled. When Jesus dies on the cross, then he can be "seen," in the Johannine sense of perceiving and acknowledging him as the only Son sent by the Father. "They will look upon him whom they have pierced" (Jn 19:37). We, too, can look at him on the cross, as did the Greeks, and let ourselves be drawn to him by the power of his love, a love to the very end.

In narrating Jesus' passion, John very clearly has his own style. He manages to let the glory shine through already in the passion itself. A striking example is the very beginning. Since the fourth gospel does not relate the agony in the garden, it starts immediately with the arrest (18:1–11). But how! It turns the arrest into a stunning victory for Jesus. First, in this critical hour, Jesus is going to spend the night in a place where he had often met with his disciples. If he wanted to escape his passion, he would have gone to some other place where he could not so easily be found. But Jesus is in no way running away from the painful implications of his mission. "This is why the Father loves me, because I lay down my life in order to take it up again. No one takes it from me, but I lay it down on my own. I have power to lay it down, and power to take it up again. This command I have received from my Father" (Jn 10:17–18). Then the band of soldiers and guards come with lanterns and torches to search for Jesus. We remember that in John's gospel Jesus is called several times "the light of the world." Such an irony. What the cohort is doing is like using a flashlight to seek the sun shining in its full force.

John also mentions explicitly that Jesus knows everything that is going to happen to him. Jesus does not wait nervously for his captors to close in on him, but he goes out to them himself. In doing so, he confronts them twice with *the* question of John's gospel: "Whom are you looking for?" (cf. Jn 1:38 and 20:15). The highlight of the scene is that Jesus also pronounces twice the momentous words, "I AM." With these two small words he identifies himself with Yahweh and once again claims his oneness with the Ineffable. As if to emphasize this climax, the soldiers in response turn away and fall to the ground. It is like a prostration before they actually arrest Jesus. What a glorious captive! Then, while he himself is in utmost danger, he cares for his disciples. He remains the good shepherd till the very end! "If you are looking for me," he tells the soldiers, "let these men go." Not only does he protect his own, he also defends the high priest's servant Malchus against Peter's inappropriate impetuosity.

The whole portrayal of the arrest is such that Jesus does not come across at all as a pitiful down-and-out wretch, but very much as magnificent in his passion.

Though John is undoubtedly the evangelist who most stresses the glory in the passion, this emphasis is by no means completely absent in the synoptics. Consider one passage from Matthew and one from Luke so as to savor how each in his own way lets the light of the resurrection shine on the suffering Jesus.

In Matthew's gospel Jesus, after his arrest, is immediately brought before the Sanhedrin, convened under the leadership of the high priest Caiaphas (26:59–68). Many false witnesses came forward, "but Jesus was silent." To remain silent under such false accusations is a remarkable sign of strength. Then the official authority—the high priest—rises to ask Jesus, under oath before the living God, about his identity: "Are you the Messiah, the Son of God?" The answer of Jesus is a climax of majestic self-awareness and serene courage. Jesus replies with two quotations from the Old Testament; in doing so he speaks exactly the language of the elders, chief priests and scribes who constituted the Sanhedrin. They are extremely familiar with every dot and iota of scripture, often using its very words in their speech. The first quotation is from the prophet Daniel (7:9–14). It is very appropriate indeed: a vision where God presides over a court and speaks a sentence about someone "like a son of man" who is led before him. The sentence, however, is startling and not at all the verdict the Sanhedrin has in mind.

> As I watched, thrones were set up and the Ancient One took his throne. His clothing was snow bright, and the hair on his head as white as wool; his throne was flames of fire, with wheels of burning fire...The court was convened, and the books were opened...As the visions during the night continued, I saw one like a son of man coming, on the clouds of heaven; when he reached the Ancient One and was presented before him, he received dominion, glory, and kingship; nations and people of every language serve him. His dominion is an everlasting dominion that shall not be taken away, his kingship shall not be destroyed.

Jesus' answer weaves the opening verse of Psalm 110 into Daniel's text. "The Lord's revelation to my Master: 'Sit on my right: your foes I will put beneath your feet.'" The message is abundantly clear. It conveys a majestic serenity in this hostile court setting, where the death sentence is a foregone conclusion.

The Sanhedrin understood the message very well. Their response to this lofty self-concept is physical abuse: "They spat in his face and struck him, while some slapped him, saying, 'Prophesy for us, Messiah: who is it that struck you?'" Rarely does such a sovereign self-definition and such a mean reaction of the official leaders come so close together. We drop sharply from one of the highpoints of the gospel into an abyss of coarseness. The glory of Jesus stands out conspicuously.

In Luke's way of the cross there are several instances where the splendor of Jesus lights up in the midst of his humiliation (23: 27–43). The first encounter is with the women who mourned and lamented him. We all know how physical pain tends to absorb our complete attention, almost to the point of obsession. It is there, right in our body, and we can neither ignore nor forget it. We may be tempted to talk endlessly about it to those who are willing to listen. Injustice done to us can obsess us even more; it is all we can think of, and we are unable to escape it. Sometimes even after many years, people still talk about it with an intense emotion as if it happened just yesterday. After having been scourged, Jesus was carrying his cross which was undoubtedly causing excruciating pain. His sentence was utterly unfair and the result of much dishonest maneuvering. So Jesus really had plenty of physical and mental pain. Yet, when the women of Jerusalem lament him, he shifts the attention away from himself to them and their children. In the midst of his anguish, he remains selflessly loving without a trace of egocentrism.

He displays no bitterness, no self-pity, no desire for revenge when his executioners nail him on the cross. Rather he says, "Father, forgive them, they know not what they do." In this prayer Jesus' magnanimity becomes evident. The glory in the passion.

The two criminals crucified with Jesus experience the same scene as he does: one of hatred, fanaticism, merciless cruelty. They also hear Jesus' merciful prayer. Their reactions to this contrast are most divergent. The one reviles Jesus while the other one asks to be remembered when Jesus comes into his kingdom. The response is majestic: "Amen, I say to you, today you will be with me in Paradise." The dying Jesus still has power over eternal destiny. Once more the glory of the crucified shines forth brilliantly.

There are many more examples of the splendor flashing radiantly out of the depth of the passion. By no means do they make the suffering less agonizing; however, they do help us to meditate on the passion in the right perspective; i.e., by never losing sight of the intrinsic and indissoluble unity of the two sides of the paschal mystery. We do not just contemplate the passion of Jesus, we contemplate the paschal mystery, of which the passion is an essential part.

23. Traces of the Passion in the Glory

On the resurrection side of the paschal mystery the vestiges of the passion and death are eternalized and can never be overlooked. The risen Lord always carries in his glorious body the nailmarks and the scar on his breast. They are signs of his dignity, the emblems of his love to the very end. They shine like jewels. The book of Revelation (5:6) captures this paradox in the image of the lamb with the slaughter wound which is yet standing on its four feet.

In most of the appearances of the risen Jesus to his disciples during the forty days after Easter, the marks of the passion are conspicuous. The linkage of death and resurrection is always the heart of his healing approach, when the glorified Lord comforts his downcast friends. Two appearances illustrate this most clearly: the one on the Road to Emmaus, and the one to Thomas in the company of the other disciples. In both we find the same basic pattern. As we reflect on them, let us place ourselves at the Easter-side of the tunnel and, standing in that bright and joyous light, see through the tunnel the profile of the cross. May we absorb so much consolation that we can generously share it with many people (cf. 2 Cor 1:3–4).

Healed from Gloom

To appreciate Luke's message more fully (Lk 24:13–35), we need to situate this passage in the context of his whole gospel, even including the Acts of the Apostles. As is well known, the third evangelist construes his gospel as one great journey towards Jerusalem; the Acts, then spread out from Jerusalem, throughout Judea and Samaria and to the ends of the earth. Jerusalem is the turning point. In the gospel it is the city of destiny: "When the days for his being taken up were fulfilled, Jesus resolutely determined to journey to Jerusalem, and he sent messengers ahead of him" (Lk 9:51–52). In Acts, Jerusalem is the starting point for the mission which is to encompass the whole world. The gospel is centripetal, Acts is centrifugal.

Moreover, it is interesting to note that in both books Mary stands at the beginning, as the Mother of Jesus and as the Mother of the church, respectively. "The angel said to Mary, 'The holy Spirit will come upon you, and the power of the Most High will overshadow you. Therefore the child to be born will be called holy, the son of God'" (Lk 1:35). In anticipation of the coming of the Spirit and the birth of the church, "all these disciples devoted themselves with one accord to prayer, together with some women, and Mary, the mother of Jesus, and his brothers" (Acts 1:14). Jerusalem is the place where IT took place, "it" being the paschal mystery, completed in Pentecost: "Stay in the city until you are clothed with power from on high" (Lk 24:49). If we look more closely, we find that Jesus' journey really ends outside the city of Jerusalem in the hands of his Father: "Jesus cried out in a loud voice, 'Father, into your hands I commend my spirit,' and when he had said this, he breathed his last" (Lk 23:46).

What John in his gospel calls "the hour" seems to be roughly equivalent to Luke's geographical designation. In the vision of the latter Jerusalem, of course, stands for the church, which is born from the Passover and in which the paschal mystery lives on among us. "Do this in memory of me."

These preliminary remarks should give us enough background to contemplate fruitfully on what happened on the road to Emmaus. Two disciples were going from Jerusalem to the village of Emmaus, and that *before* the paschal mystery was completed (cf. 24:49). So they are on the wrong track; or more accurately, they may be on the right road, but are going in the wrong direction. The movement of the gospel is still *towards* Jerusalem, yet they go away from it. They are like ghost riders. They have overlooked the salient signs "Do not enter. Wrong way." They are a danger for other people on the road. They have gone astray and are lost. Some exegetes think they are not just lost sheep, but lost shepherds: "Shepherds in the mist."

The chief shepherd goes after them. On the very day of the resurrection, the hero of the day is not looking for huge crowds and great publicity, but quietly takes his time for two people who desperately need his help. It is the economy of the good shepherd who, having a hundred sheep and losing one of them, leaves the ninety-nine in the desert to go after the lost one until he finds it. It is the economy of heaven, where there is more joy over one sinner who repents than over ninety-nine righteous people who have no need of repentance (cf. Lk 15:4,7). "I have called you by name; you are mine....You are precious in my eyes and...I love you" (Is 43:1,4). Each one of you!

A good pastor meets his people where they are. These two are sad. They are still in the passion. They have not left the cross. They have not progressed at all; now they are even regressing. The disappointment of Calvary has stunted their growth. Since their great hope has been dashed, there has been no further spiritual development.

They had believed in Jesus. Wholeheartedly, they had given themselves to him and become his disciples. They had given up everything for him according to the challenging word of the Master: "Everyone of you who does not renounce all possessions cannot be my disciple" (Lk 14:33). The two felt they had really met Jesus' call. They had recognized in him the Messiah. They were thrilled that the reign of God had come in Jesus, that there was going to be liberty for the captives and sight for the blind, as Jesus had announced in the synagogue of Nazareth. Yes, they expected everything from him, all that the prophets had promised.

Then, in the passion of Jesus, their whole world broke down. They were disappointed, truly shattered. Their mistake, though, was not that they had expected too much, but rather that they had the wrong picture of how it would come about. Yet, Jesus had spoken unambiguously about his suffering to come. And so had the prophets, and the Songs of the Servant of Yahweh, that outline of Jesus' mission. But they had overheard it all, or heard and thoroughly repressed it.

These disciples had conjured up ambitious, grandiose plans for the reign of God. That was all right but in those plans there was no room for the cross. That was a fatal omission.

So when the cross actually came, they were not at all prepared. Their faith collapsed, and they quit. Suffering can become a spiritual setback, and even a source of infidelity, if we are not able to integrate it into our relationship with Jesus. It can as well deepen our faith and our commitment, on the condition that we manage to give it its proper place in our union with Christ. In the latter case "all things will work for our good," as Paul boldly states (Rom 8:28). If we can bring everything before God, there will be no losses in the gospel.

On the other hand, sufferings and disappointments easily lead to gloom and self-pity, bitterness and disloyalty if they are not shared with Jesus. In that frame of mind we most likely shall become soft on ourselves and seek compensations, which make us lose more and more our first love (cf. Rev 2:4). If we do not know how to give the cross its rightful place, there is a real danger of falling into pettiness and shallowness.

That is exactly what Cleopas and his companion did not manage to do. That plunged them into depression and caused them to leave the community of the disciples. Then the risen Lord came to their rescue. First, he let them verbalize at length their disappointments. They are only too eager to expose "the sort of things that had happened to Jesus the Nazarene," but at the end of their eloquent list of occurrences they leave out the resurrection. That is a vital oversight because the latter would have changed completely the perspective of all the foregoing. That is the exact reason why they are downcast.

That is also the precise point where Jesus commences his healing. He accepts all the facts that are so troublesome to them, and then puts them in the new context. Jesus does not deny anything; rather he just progresses a little further, and in doing so changes the whole picture thoroughly. He connects the passion-side of the tunnel where the two disciples stand with the Easter-side; immediately the stream of light shines through and transforms the scene completely.

The paschal mystery integrates the gruesome passion and makes it fruitful: "Was it not necessary that the Messiah should suffer these things and enter into his glory? Then, beginning with Moses and all the prophets, he interpreted to them what referred to him in all the Scriptures." With that, the two were healed. Their despondent hearts started to burn like never before.

They urged the stranger to stay with them, since the day was almost over. But when he disappeared from their eyes after they recognized him in the breaking of the bread, it was not too late for them to go all the way to Jerusalem and to join the disciples whom they had deserted. They felt an inner urge to return to the community. Itching as they were to share their experience, they first had to listen to the eleven and their companions: "The Lord has truly been raised and has appeared to Simon." Then they too could recount what had taken place on the way. That is the epitome of church: sharing with one another the faith in the risen Lord, and helping each other to perceive everything in that perspective.

Healed from Stubbornness

On that same evening, in John's gospel, we find the disciples together behind locked doors "for fear of the Jews" (20:19–31). The good news of the resurrection has not as yet transformed their hearts. They do not up to this time have the deep inner security necessary to reach out as witnesses. They do not yet dare to venture out and to proclaim the gospel of the risen Lord. How often in the history of the Christian community has this situation repeated itself—individuals or groups who locked themselves in for fear? How often have we yielded to the temptation not to stick our necks out because we were fearful?

Then, the risen Lord suddenly stands in the midst of their fear. That is typical of Jesus: he came into our midst in the incarnation. He went into the midst of our sin in his extreme solidarity with us, when he received his baptism with those who "were being baptized by John in the Jordan river as they acknowledged their sins" (Mt 3:6). He went into the midst of death, sharing with us the ultimate loneliness so that we may meet him there and no longer be cut off in the end. He overcame sin, he overcame death, he overcame fear. He is our savior.

Twice he greets them with the traditional Jewish salutation: "Shalom!" However, when the risen Lord speaks this word, it is no longer the ordinary greeting. It conveys that peace he once talked about (Jn 14:27), which the world cannot give nor take away. It is the peace which dispels undue fear, and ends anxious isolation.

The gesture that expresses this peace is the showing of his hands and side: the risen Lord displaying the marks of his wounds! This captures the paschal mystery in a simple gesture, which presents the two sides of the pasch in one posture. Nothing can better convey the peace of the reign of God than the risen Jesus showing the breast scar and the nailmarks in his glorified body.

Jesus then speaks these important words: "As the Father has sent me, so I send you." He transmits to his disciples and to us that which formed the essence of his life—his mission by the Father (cf. ch.7). "When he has said this, he breathed on them"—on each of them, just as God breathed the breath of life into the clay which he had molded when he created *ha'adam* (Gen 2:7). In doing so, "Jesus said to them, 'Receive the Holy Spirit.'" It is in this Spirit that Jesus fulfilled his own mission; as the fruit of his consummated mission, Jesus now can give us this same Holy Spirit to enable us to accomplish our mission. The crown of Jesus' mission was to forgive our sins; his name was Jesus, because he was to "save his people from their sins" (Mt 1:21). The Holy Spirit enables the disciples to do the same: "Whose sins you forgive are forgiven and whose sins you retain are retained." The divine prerogative is shared with the community. It is the origin of the sacrament of reconciliation, Jesus' Easter gift to his church.

This episode is unique in the Bible. The risen Lord confers on the disciples the power to forgive sins. God's love has two extremes, like two hands with which it reaches out to us. The one hand is the resurrection: God does not abandon us in our dying, but holds us in and beyond our death. The other hand is the forgiveness: God does not let us down in our guilt, but there also love's mighty hand keeps accepting us. The two hands stretched out to us meet us precisely in the two extreme situations, where our own strength falls short—death and guilt. The beauty of this passage in John's gospel is that these two extreme forms of God's love meet here—the resurrection and the forgiveness of sins.

Yet there is one large shadow on this magnificent event on Easter evening: "Thomas, called the Twin, one of the twelve, was not with them when Jesus came." Thomas is still with the suffering Jesus. He may have anticipated the passion earlier than the other disciples. With his keen perceptiveness he realized sooner than the other eleven that the forces of the establishment were too strong to be overthrown by Jesus. He foresaw that Jesus was heading for disaster. He already saw the cross looming on the horizon when the other apostles were still naively savoring the extraordinary popularity of their master. From that time onward, his enthusiasm wilts, his fervor peters out, and his generosity declines. The idealist turns into a pessimist. And when the passion actually does take place, his reaction is ambiguous. On the one hand he shares with the others an acute disappointment and a deep sense of pain. On the other hand the crucifixion proved that he was right in his lonely opinion, and therefore was a confirmation of his stance. He certainly was, no less than the disciples of Emmaus, mired in the passion and unable to move on to the joy of the resurrection. He remains obstinate in rejecting the witness of the other ten.

His big words and unheard-of conditions indicate how bogged down he really is. His stubbornness, though, is not a sign of insensitivity but rather the reaction of a super-sensitive person, who is so deeply disappointed that he seeks protection behind a facade of toughness. In his predicament he retreats more and more into a self-created loneliness. His isolation is enhanced, because the others are not able to interpret his obstinacy correctly.

Jesus does not leave him alone in his crisis. He is going to heal him, but in the community with the other apostles. That point is very significant. It is in and through the church, which is his body, that Jesus is present and active. Once in the group, Thomas is invited to touch the wounds in Jesus' hands and side, as he had demanded in his stubborn isolation. It is not that Jesus wants him to eat his words and embarrass him. There is no vindictiveness in the risen Lord. Jesus wants to liberate him from his gloomy self-inflicted confinement, and to usher him into the joy and the vastness of the resurrection. As with Cleopas and his companion, the good shepherd once again meets the stray sheep where it is—entrenched in the passion. So he lets Thomas touch the wounds. That is where Thomas feels at home. Jesus is conveying to him: "You were right. The crucifixion did come. It was horrible. Feel it. Put your finger in the nailmarks and your hand into my side. It is all so terribly real. Yes, Thomas, you have seen it coming correctly."

For the first time since Good Friday, Thomas relaxes. Finally, at long last, here is someone who does not corner him and drive him still deeper into his painful isolation. But then this relief is only the prelude to a far deeper change. He now discovers that the marks of the crucifixion, on which he had been focusing so obsessively, have a completely unexpected context. They are parts of the risen body. They share in its radiance.

For Thomas this is the breakthrough out of his isolation. The wounds are integrated into the resurrected body; the passion is integrated into the paschal mystery; his own distress is integrated into the wide scope of the good news. He bursts out of his prison. Light and happiness flow in overwhelmingly. His resistance is overcome. With eager conviction now he can say his profession of faith, "My Lord and my God." The paschal mystery has healed another victim of a one-sided view.

The final words of Jesus are meant not only for Thomas, but for all the faithful of the Johannine community, and for all the readers of John's gospel through the ages. Twenty chapters have worked up to this climax. Matthew has eight beatitudes at the beginning of his gospel. John has one in the middle, after the washing of the disciples' feet. It is the beatitude of love: Blessed are you if you do as I did to you (cf. Jn 13:17). He concludes his gospel with his second beatitude—the beatitude of faith: "Blessed are those who have not seen and have believed." To lead us to this faith, John wrote his gospel: "These signs are written that you may believe that Jesus is the Messiah, the Son of God, and that through this belief you may have life in his name."

VII

THE GIFT OF GRATEFULNESS

24. The Giver in the Gift

✦

Gratefulness

Gratefulness[1] creates a positive attitude toward life and opens a joyful way to find God in everything. Grateful people are pleasant people whom we all like to be with. They are people who make life happier and richer—their own lives, *and* the lives of others. They are people who do not lose courage in difficult circumstances, but keep their hearts alert against the dark forces which tend to bog us down. We do not have to worry about the mental health of those for whom gratefulness has become second nature. One cannot at the same time be grateful and unhappy. On the other hand, ungrateful people can render life miserable: they stifle so much good.

In the gospel we read that Jesus was a grateful person, a man of thankfulness. He showed gratitude for the big and little things of life: for a cup of water from the Samaritan as well as for the friendship which he found with Mary, Martha, and Lazarus. He said a prayer of gratitude before each meal, but also before he raised Lazarus from the tomb. He thanked his Father in the words of the psalms, and also spontaneously in his own words. Filled with joy, he would bless and thank his Father (cf. Lk 10:21).

He was grateful for the flowers in the fields and the birds in the air, for the sun that rises and for the rains that fall. Deep in his heart he realized that life, that every life, that *his* life is a gift. He knew that he was called by his Abba, "my delight" and that God was well pleased with him (Mt 3:17).

165

Jesus tried to respond to this relationship. His life had been given him by his Abba and he lived life to the full only when he accomplished the will of his Abba. This was the food on which he lived. "My food is to do the will of the one who sent me, and to finish his work" (Jn 4:34). In other words, the gratefulness of Jesus was never noncommittal, never just a feeling or lip service, but it did shape his life.

The Jewish tradition has a saying: "Whoever enjoys anything in this world without first saying a prayer or a blessing commits an untruthfulness." These words from the Talmud refer to the beginning of Psalm 24, "The Lord's is the earth and its fullness." Only through a berakah (blessing) a man or a woman receives the right to use the goods of the earth; without such a blessing the use of them is dishonest. Therefore, the Jewish tradition knows many berakot also for very profane things! Moreover the Jews pray three times a day: "We thank you for your miracles which are daily with us and for your continual marvels." Many psalms stress gratefulness: "Pay your sacrifice of thanksgiving to God; a sacrifice of thanksgiving honors me" (Ps 50:14, 23). "My soul, give thanks to the Lord and never forget all his blessings" (Ps 103:1–2).

Mary and Joseph raised the child Jesus in this tradition. They taught him first to thank and bless God before enjoying anything, and Jesus was a keen pupil. He interiorized these lessons fully. We sense in his public life how spontaneous and deep-seated his thankfulness was.

Not only the Jewish but also the Christian tradition has something to say about gratefulness. Through many centuries all our prefaces have begun with the appeal: "Let us give thanks to the Lord our God," and most of them start with the words, "Father, it is our duty and our salvation always and everywhere to give you thanks." The original Latin expression says even more forcefully, "to *do* thanks": gratitude is something we do, always and everywhere.

The center and climax of our prayer and liturgy is the eucharist. The Greek word *eucharist* means precisely the celebration of gratitude. On certain days we say or sing in the liturgy the Gloria, with these words: "We give you thanks for your glory." Thanksgiving, then, becomes adoration. Thanksgiving happens not just with the tongue and the head, but also with the heart and the hand; it encompasses the whole person.

Toward the end of the liturgical year the people of the United States traditionally celebrate Thanksgiving Day. It is a legal holiday, which has a special place in the hearts of everyone and is observed with great warmth and conviction. It is truly a wonderful feast, with deep roots in the Judeo-Christian tradition.

The New Testament speaks often of gratitude. An example is this verse from St. Paul, "Everything indeed is for you, so that the grace bestowed on more and more people may cause the thanksgiving to overflow for the glory of God" (2 Cor 4:15). In this passage Paul talks about all the troubles and trials of his apostolate. He accepts everyone of them for a double reason which eventually turns into one: the salvation of people and the abundance of thanksgiving. In his earliest letter Paul writes succinctly: "In all circumstances give thanks, for this is the will of God for you in Christ Jesus" (1 Thes 5:18).

One example from the later Christian tradition is the beginning of a letter of St. Ignatius of Loyola to one of his first companions, Simon Rodriguez:

> It seems to me in the light of the Divine Goodness, although others may think differently, that ingratitude is the most abominable of sins and that it should be detested in the sight of our Creator and Lord by all of His creatures who are capable of enjoying His divine and everlasting glory. For it is a forgetting of the graces, benefits, and blessings received. As such it is the cause, beginning, and origin of all sins and misfortunes. On the contrary, the grateful acknowledgment of blessings and gifts received is loved and esteemed not only on earth but in heaven.[2]

Acknowledged Dependence

Gratitude can be described as acknowledged dependence—a dependence to which we say "yes." Its extreme opposite is pride, which makes us believe that we only count for what we achieve ourselves, and that we owe everything solely to ourselves; it is an illness. Gratitude recognizes that I receive something, and consequently am dependent on the other person who gave it to me or did it for me, and that I acknowledge and express this dependence. There are some independent characters who have great trouble acknowledging just this. If one gives them a gift, their first reaction is to estimate the price of that gift; then the next week they will send a present of about the same value or probably a bit more: thus the balance is restored. Such people cannot stand to owe anything to anyone!

Yet everything I have and am is received from others: the language I speak, the house I live in, the freedom I enjoy, my thinking, my faith, it all comes through others to me. Gratitude means to acknowledge that I am not the origin of my own being and of all that I need for my being. Gratefulness recognizes in a positive way what others do and mean for me.

We must *learn* to live with a grateful heart, because in each of us there is also a tendency to ascribe everything to ourselves or to take things for granted. From the beginning the Jewish people were educated to gratefulness. Moses teaches the Israelites in the book of Deuteronomy:

> It was not because you are the largest of all nations that the Lord set his heart on you and chose you, for you are really the smallest of all nations (7.7).

> Otherwise, you might say to yourselves, "It is my own power and the strength of my own hand that has obtained for me this wealth." Remember then, it is the Lord, your God, who gives you the power to acquire wealth, by fulfilling, as he has now done, the covenant which he swore to your fathers (8:17–18).

> Understand this, therefore: it is not because of your merits that the Lord, your God, is giving you this good land to possess, for you are a stiff-necked people (9:6).

In the New Testament we find a similar teaching; for example, when Paul reminds his Corinthians:

> Consider your own calling. Not many of you were wise by human standards, not many were powerful, not many were of noble birth. Rather God chose the foolish of the world to shame the wise and God chose the weak of the world to shame the strong, and God chose the lowly and despised of the world, those who count for nothing, to reduce to nothing those who are something; so that no human being might boast before God (1 Cor 1:26–29).

Acknowledging our dependence calls for a certain maturity. A *child* rejoices over a gift without troubling itself about where the gift comes from; a child has no problem believing in Santa Claus, as long as the gifts land with the right person, i.e. me. A child must learn to say thank you; spontaneously it does not think of doing this. Likewise, a child will never say, "that is really too much," or "there is no need to give me that much," or "can you really spare this?" That is the language of adults. Children receive without questioning the gifts offered them.

The *adolescent*, on the other hand, realizes where things come from, but frequently finds it difficult to acknowledge that dependence. This leads repeatedly to inharmonious and even unfair behavior, which can really hurt others. Of course, adolescence is not to be measured in chronological age. A mentality that focuses exclusively on the rights one has or demands relentlessly what can only be given freely, stymies gratefulness. It shows a lack of maturity.

An *adult* has come to terms with his or her limitations and dependence, and therefore is able to acknowledge and accept with a thankful heart. That is why mature gratefulness can easily develop into a religious attitude, recognizing God as the source of all good and wanting to reciprocate in service and surrender. The adult has discovered and interiorized that the greatest values of life can neither be purchased nor achieved. That which gives our life depth and peace is far more gift than accomplishment: love, faith, prayer, fidelity, friendship, forgiveness, inner security, hope, good health...

In the "Contemplation to Attain Love" at the end of the Spiritual Exercises, the retreatant is encouraged to pray for "interior knowledge of all the great good I have received, in order that, stirred to profound gratitude, I may become able to love and serve the divine majesty in all things" (233). The awareness of the many blessings received leads to an authentic service of the Lord. Gratitude does not limit itself to feelings and words, but expresses itself also in deeds; again, this mature gratitude is something each of us must learn, rehearse, and practice.

Dorothy Sölle wrote in one of her books that she caught herself thanking and praising God very little in recent years. In her manifold activities, gratitude tended to fade away. She realized that this was a great loss, and decided from then on not to go to bed without having thanked God for three specific things of the past day. I know a confrere who, inspired by Sölle's example, bought himself a tiny notebook; each evening he writes three concrete things of the past day for which he is grateful. This booklet turns out to be a great help especially on dark days; just glancing through its pages cheers him up. Brother David Steindl Rast, OSB, mentions that for years he has written in his pocket calendar each day at least one new thing for which he has not as yet been grateful. Perhaps someone fears it might be difficult each day to find a new motive for gratefulness. From his own experience, Brother David tells us it is not; on the contrary, often four or five motives present themselves. "I cannot imagine how old I must become before I noticeably exhaust the stock."

Gratitude Implies Trust

Unless I trust a person, I cannot be truly thankful toward that person. If I receive a gift and fear that somehow it might have been stolen, I cannot really enjoy it; perhaps soon the police will be after me. Or, more realistically, if somebody whom I do not fully trust gives me a present, I may well think, now this person gives me this but possibly next week the same person will ask me to do something and put some pressure on me because of the gift given. I won't feel free enough to turn down the request. Through the gift, I have to some extent become dependent on that person. When I harbor these thoughts or feelings in my head or my heart, I cannot enjoy the gift anymore.

Gratitude celebrates the bond that binds giver and receiver. But sometimes the bond is such that it cannot be celebrated. Some persons I just do not trust enough to be dependent upon.

Thankfulness means that I allow somebody into my life. A real "present" renders the giver "present" in my life. That is, after all, why the giver gives his gift—in order to be present to the other person. To truly accept a gift, is to admit the giver. Suppose a good friend, returning from a vacation in Switzerland, gives me a pocketknife from that country. Whenever I use it, it reminds me of him and I rejoice over our friendship. It makes him present to me.

However, this will only happen when the giver really puts him or herself into the gift. A little incident, which I read some time ago in a magazine, illustrates the point well. Admittedly, it is rather sentimental; but it is also quite on target. Every Thursday an elderly woman in a nursing home receives a beautiful bouquet from her daughter, who lives at a distance. The mother is delighted and always puts the flowers on a table in the middle of her room. She leaves the door open, hoping that someone will notice the flowers and comment on them. That will give her an opportunity to talk about her daughter. On her birthday the daughter flies in to spend the day with her. The mother thanks her daughter in glowing terms for her attentiveness. The daughter feels a little embarrassed and dampens the mother's joy by revealing that the flowers are simply a standing order on her account. The following Thursday the flowers arrive as usual. The mother puts them on the dresser and leaves the door just half open. The bouquet has lost some of its meaningfulness because the giver is less present in the gift than the mother had mistakenly assumed.

The gift's full stature can also be stunted, because the receiver does not do justice to it. One who skims a gift book briefly and then puts it permanently on the shelf is not really grateful.

Lack of attention is the epitome of ungratefulness. Taking every-thing for granted stifles all gratitude. A grateful person lives more attentively. Gratitude gives access to genuine humanism; it lies at the root of culture. Grateful people appreciate the past and care for the future.

25. Finding God in Everything

Transparency

Let us return briefly to the example of the gift of the pocket-knife and stretch it a little in order to make an important point. Suppose my friend and I become estranged and our friendship ends. Now in my mind I can separate the knife from the giver. It is just a simple mental process. What remains is no longer a present, but just a handy pocketknife. That's all.

The example (admittedly somewhat farfetched) illustrates a key difference in outlook. The believer can experience everything as gift in which the giver is present. Things, situations, people acquire a kind of fullness. They carry a richness within themselves, a reference to the goodness of the giver. We discover that there is a mystery in all that exists, its "Deepest Ground." On the other hand, one can also look upon things, and even people, in a business-like fashion, evaluating them by their utility and efficiency, and leaving it at that.

The way things and people function depends to a great extent on our attitude toward them. We can approach them with reverence and a sense of wonder, so that their inner secret is respected and the Other in them recognized and reverenced. We can also deprive them of their depth, cut them loose from their roots, and reduce their significance.

Only in thankfulness do things and people stand out and are

rightly appreciated. Only in gratitude do they have a chance to be fully themselves. That is why one can argue that being thankful is having a realistic attitude toward life. It gives reality its rightful scope. A person who does not know how to be thankful truncates reality and flattens the world. Someone who can neither experience nor express gratitude lacks a basic prerequisite for good mental health. That is why some psychiatrists try to enhance the sense of thankfulness in their clients.

We know that a grieving process is needed to digest a loss. Similarly, thankfulness is needed to digest the positive and absorb the richness of what is received. Giving thanks completes the giving. Without thanks, the giving has not fully taken place. There is a danger of losing oneself so completely in the gift that one forgets the giver. Ascetism is important, not in the first place because we might abuse the gifts, but more so to keep a sufficient distance. Only then shall we be able to recognize the "Beyond" in the gifts and thus do them full justice. Thankfulness gives life its depth and perspective; it makes reality lucid and transparent. It is through thankfulness that people and their world become more harmonious.

Thankfulness means tracing things back to the source from whence they have come. Thankfulness opens the entrance to the core of things. Only in that way can a person be rooted in reality, confirmed in one's existence. Ignatius used to call it "finding God in all things." Thankfulness transforms things and events into a piece of the mosaic of God's love story with humankind, into an instant of salvation history.

All that exists is God's gift. The Almighty invests the divine love in every nook and cranny of creation. What is, is given, i.e., it is communicated; it is bestowed in order to be received. "Love consists in a mutual communication...," Ignatius remarks (Sp Ex 231). In his high priestly prayer, Jesus says to the Father: "Everything of mine is yours and everything of yours is mine" (Jn 17:10). That expresses complete trust, unconditional abandonment, fullness of love, perfect communication.

Gratitude Goes Out to Someone

We all know the embarrassment that accompanies an anonymous present. It is nice to be surprised with a gift and we appreciate the unobtrusiveness of the giver, but it is frustrating not to be able to thank that person. We feel like saying "thank you" to anyone who might possibly be the giver, yet that could create awkward situations, because people will think we had expected something from them. So we cannot express our gratitude, and that is quite inhibiting.

In his biography of St. Francis, Chesterton remarks that the worst moment for the atheist is when he or she is really thankful and has nobody to thank.[1] That must be the same inhibiting experience on a much larger scale.

One can hardly be grateful to an institution either. Certainly there does exist something like an anonymous thankfulness. We can be grateful for living in a free country, for our family traditions, for medical progress, for the good spirit in our parish or community, for our education, and many other communal values. We know that many people contributed to these blessings, though they may be unknown to us. That is anonymous gratitude. Yet full-fledged thankfulness has always specific persons in mind. And in the last analysis, we believe it is God's love and care that were incarnated in these persons' goodness. The lover who says to his or her beloved, "I thank God that you exist," is right. Our thankfulness falls short if it does not extend to God.

Gratefulness is finding the right connection between oneself and other persons and things. That is why it is a mature attitude. Thankfulness means on the one hand being conscious of one's own worth, and on the other hand being aware of one's dependence. Thankfulness implies a healthy self-esteem, but at the same time it is altruistic, other-directed. Self-centeredness and egotism are the archenemies of every kind of thankfulness. One who is always after his or her own interests, whose attention is always focused on self, will never be a grateful person. In like manner, the one who gets completely absorbed in the gift, while forgetting the giver, is also ungrateful. Thankfulness means that we do not see ourselves as the center of the universe, and that we do not take things for granted but as granted by God. Thankfulness does not see different things, but sees things differently. It heightens our open-mindedness and makes the world more transparent.

There is a certain similarity between thankfulness and an artistic sense. Taste for art brings joy and delight. It makes us savor the beauty of things. So does thankfulness. It seems that the joy of the grateful heart is deeper and more encompassing than the enjoyment of art. Perhaps we can call the joy of thankfulness, peace. And if our thankfulness goes out to God, it is a peace which the world cannot give.

Grateful people are delightful. They are bringers of good news. I remember visiting a woman in a nursing home who had suffered the last twelve years from multiple sclerosis. She was in a wheelchair and her left hand was completely paralyzed. She told me how she initially had revolted against her illness. But gradually she had learned to accept and to make the most of it. During our conversation her eyes suddenly lit up as she said with great conviction, "Father, I am so grateful that I can still use my right hand." I was deeply moved. A little bit of heaven opened up in the midst of much suffering. I felt ashamed for having seldom, if ever, thanked God for my two healthy hands. Unique as the encounter was for me, I am sure that many people have had similar experiences, perhaps even more striking.

Thankfulness does not belittle, but rather lets things and people shine to full advantage. Neither do thankful people belittle themselves. The attitude of thankfulness and an inferiority complex are not compatible. Anthony de Mello stated: "It is inconceivable that anybody could be grateful and unhappy.[2] The German psychiatrist Albert Görres observes the same incompatibility: "one cannot be discontented and thankful at the same time."[3] We touch here again on the therapeutic quality of thankfulness: it fosters wholeness. When people have a strongly developed sense of gratitude, there is no need to worry about their mental and spiritual health. Our Lady exemplifies this beautifully. Her Magnificat bears witness to her articulate self-esteem (great things done to her, all generations will call her blessed), and to a profound recognition of God (the Almighty has done this to me, he has shown the strength of his arm, holy is his name). Thankfulness is not confined in self-sufficiency and self-conceit, but rather acknowledges in everything the source transcending us.

To make this more practical, consider the case of someone who experiences great success and, because of that, receives much honor and praise. That could create a problem of vainglory. At the very beginning of his autobiography, Ignatius mentions how he wrestled with this temptation. The real problem, though, is not that one receives recognition, but that one lets this recognition stop with oneself, and does not pursue it to its ultimate source. Once we recognize our successes and honors as originating from God, we can fully enjoy them without pride or vainglory.[4] Once again, thankfulness teaches us perspective and a healthy balance, in this instance of being at the same time humble and happy.

Thankfulness requires a certain distance. When obsessed by the gift, we forget the giver. When we are overly attached to something, we are neither free enough to be genuinely grateful nor can we really enjoy it. It is also impossible to be thankful for what has been thrust upon us. Conversely, gratefulness creates a certain distance which prevents us from being crushed by what we receive. This is another wholesome fruit of thankfulness.

Gratitude means to pay attention, not only to the gift and to the giver, but also to the giving. A grateful person is heedful and alert. Thankfulness gauges our liveliness. Seneca puts it this way:

> Ungrateful is one who denies a kindness done to oneself.
> Ungrateful is the person who covers it up.
> Ungrateful is the person who does not respond.
> Most ungrateful of all is the one who forgets.[5]

To forget can be a serious wrong; *can* be, I wrote; it *need* not be serious. Sometimes it is just harmless and accidental. But there is also a forgetting that is the result of an egocentric way of life, or of an obsession or addiction. It may be caused by repression or projection. To some people we cannot be grateful in any real way, because we do not admit them into our lives.

To be forgotten can be terrible. In the Old Testament the worst thing one can do to a person is to forget that person. The psalmist prays to God: "Will your wonders be known in the dark or your justice in the land of oblivion?" (88:13).

To acknowledge what is repressed is therapeutic. That is where gratitude comes in again. An ungrateful person experiences everything as a burden and a duty, as fate and coercion, threat and disaster. Gratitude presents a different perspective, makes room and sets free.

The Memory of the Heart

A grateful person commemorates the independence of a country and those who gave their lives for it, a birthday of loved ones, and the anniversary of a wedding and of a dear friend's death. A grateful person celebrates the *magnalia Dei*, God's marvelous deeds, above all, the death of Jesus in connection with his resurrection. Eucharist is memory turned into gratitude. In his farewell discourse Jesus promises us the Holy Spirit to remind us (cf. Jn 14:26).

"Blessed are the pure of heart, for they shall see God" (Mt 5:8). The undivided heart makes things, situations, and people transparent; it sees through them. It recognizes in them the Deepest Ground, the mystery in the heart of all that is, ultimately the love of our Abba in heaven. The pure heart is not greedy, and does not grab; it is not enslaved and not possessive; it is not dissipated and bored; it looks beyond mere utility or self-advantage; it is not fixated on achievement and accomplishment. To live singleheartedly makes it so much easier to live a thankful, prayerful life, and to find God at work in it (cf. Jn 5:17).

In biblical vocabulary, heart denotes the profound and authentic reality of the human being, in opposition to the appearance and semblance. The heart is the mysterious spring of our life energy. "More than all else, keep watch over your heart, since here are the wellsprings of life" (Prv 4:23 JB). Most important of all, it is in our hearts that the capacity to love resides, which unites us with the origin of all creation. The heart has an unfathomable depth, akin to God's creative love itself. For every human person it is a primary responsibility to find the way to one's heart. In this endeavor gratitude is a staunch ally.

In Luke's first chapter Mary sings her Magnificat, *the* song of thanksgiving (1:46–55). Immediately before that she spoke her "fiat" (1:38). There is a close connection between the two. Those who dare not surrender themselves can never be thankful. Surrender and thankfulness interact and strengthen each other. In the final contemplation of the Spiritual Exercises, the grace we ask for is "interior knowledge of all the great good we have received," and this contemplation flows into the closing prayer, the prayer of abandonment: "Take, Lord, and receive all my liberty..." (233). Similarly, the eucharist celebration comprises both gratitude and the gift of self.

Ultimately thankfulness means loving in return with the same love with which we are loved. By being grateful for what we have received, we are made ready for what is to be done without rashness and without faintheartedness. Thankfulness implies receptivity, but is by no means passivity. It is never noncommittal, never just a polite formula. Thankfulness transforms the gift into a task to be done and has, therefore, a "ready-to-work" attitude; not in the spirit of achievement or of becoming quits, but in order to let the gift bear fruit.

There is much in this world for which we cannot and should not be grateful. Suffering and injustice are an appeal to work patiently and tirelessly for a better world. For this long-winded task thankful people are best prepared, better than their angry or fanatical counterparts. Moreover, grateful people will more readily discover and admit that the evil is also within ourselves as a fifth column. This leads to a different attitude. Gratefully we believe that in this fight against the evil around us and in us we are instruments in God's hand and co-workers with Jesus. Thankfulness deepens the awareness of our being united and more readily lets all God's glory through.

APPENDIX

Appendix

In the account of her annual retreat, St. Therese Couderc, wrote on June 26, 1864:

Now, what is self-surrender? I well understand the full extent of the meaning of the word self-surrender, but I am unable to express it. I only know that it is very extensive, embracing the present and the future.

Self-surrender is more than being dedicated, more than giving one's self, it is even more than abandoning one's self to God. Self-surrender, then, is dying to everything and to one's self, no longer to be concerned with one's self but to keep it always turned towards God.

Self-surrender, again, is no longer to seek one's self in anything, either spiritually or physically, that is, no longer to seek self-satisfaction but solely God's good pleasure.

It should be added that self-surrender is also that spirit of detachment which prefers nothing, neither people, nor things, nor time, nor place, but which adheres to everything, accepts everything, submits to everything.

Now, this might be thought to be very difficult. That is wrong: nothing is so easy to do and nothing so enjoyable to practice. It all consists of making once and for all a generous act while saying with all the sincerity of one's soul: "My God, I want to be wholly yours, deign to accept my offering." All has been said and done. From then on, one must be careful to stay in this state of soul, and not to draw back before any small sacrifices that may help one's growth in virtue. One must recall that act of SURRENDER.

I pray to Our Lord to give an understanding of this word to all those souls desirous of pleasing Him, and to inspire them with such an easy means of sanctification. Oh! if it could be understood beforehand what sweetness and peace is tasted when no reservation is made with the good Lord! How He communicates with the soul that seeks Him sincerely and has been able to abandon itself. Let anyone try it and he will see that here is true happiness to be sought in vain elsewhere.

The self-surrendered soul has found paradise on earth since it enjoys that sweet peace which is part of the happiness of the elect.[1]

---

[1] *Annals of the Congregation of Our Lady of the Cenacle,* Vol. IV, 1856–65, p. 151f.

Notes

Unless otherwise stated the psalm quotations are taken from *Christian Prayer: The Liturgy of the Hours*. Usually other biblical quotations are from the *New American Bible*. The abbreviation JB refers to the *Jerusalem Bible*; Sp Ex to the *Spiritual Exercises of St. Ignatius of Loyola (†1556)*.

Chapter 1

1. *Parochial and Plain Sermons* in 8 volumes, Vol. III, Sermon 9; April 5, 1835. (London and New York: Longman, Green, and Co., 1907), 124f.

2. *Letters and Papers from Prison*, Revised Edition, edited by Eberhard Bethge (New York: The Macmillan Company, 1968), 188f.

3. *Theologische Gebete* (Frankfurt am Main: Josef Knecht, 1960), 12f.

4. *The Song of the Bird* (Anand, India: Gujarat Sahitya Prakash, 1982), 144f.

Chapter 2

1. Certain Protestant theologians, like Karl Barth, consider religion intrinsically as the antithesis of faith. In this tradition Dietrich Bonhoeffer looks for a "Christianity without religion."

2. For example, St. Augustine: *Cor incurvatum in seipsum*—a self-absorbed heart; St. Bonaventure: *Libertas recurvata in seipsam*—freedom constricted in itself; Martin Luther: *Homo incurvatus in seipsum*—a person tied down by self.

Chapter 3

1. In French mysticism this is called "la fine pointe de l'âme."

2. *Should Anyone Say Forever* (Chicago, Loyola University Press, 1977), 21–23.

Chapter 4

1. In this interpretation the evangelist goes beyond the literal translation of the name Jesus or Joshua, which simply means "God saves," and tapers its meaning to salvation "from their sins." Jesus stands not just for a salvation in general, but specifically for salvation from our sins. Consistent with this rendition, Matthew has Jesus say, "I did not come to call the virtuous but sinners" (Mt 9:13 JB).

2. The idea is from Bishop Paul Van den Berghe of Antwerp, Belgium.

3. Maurice Blondel, *L'Action (1893)* (Paris, Presses Universitaires de France, 1950), 330f; English translation by Olive Blanchette (Notre Dame, Indiana, 1984), 306f.

4. Cf. Andre Louf, OCSO, *Inspelen op Genade* (Tielt: Lannoo, 1983), 194–196.

Chapter 5

1. It is taken from an oratorio *Vigiles de St. Ignace*, 1991, presented on the occasion of the Ignatian jubilees 1990/91. The text is from Didier Rimaud, S.J., and this particular passage is based on Sp Ex 53.

2. Werner Bergengruen, *Der spanische Rosenstock* (Tübingen: Rainer Wunderlich Verlag, 1940), 59.

3. Twenty-Sixth Sunday in ordinary time.

Chapter 6

1. A good example is the flight of Hagar into the desert, mentioned in chapter 1 (Gen 16). In verse 7 it is said, "The Lord's messenger found Hagar by a spring in the wilderness..."; without any explicit transition, verse 13 reads, "To the Lord who spoke to her..."

2. II, A, 2.

3. *Apostolicam Actuositatem*, 2.

4. Meditations and devotions of the late Cardinal Newman (London and New York: Longmans, Green, and Co. 1907), 301.

Chapter 7

1. St. Thérèse Couderc (†1885) elaborates on this attitude which she calls self-surrender, in a text which can be found in the Appendix of this book.

2. Uomini di Pace e di Riconciliazione (Roma: Edizioni Borla, 1985), Sesta Meditazione

3. Feb. 11, 1544, #15. In: *The Classics of Western Spirituality, Ignatius of Loyola*, edited by George E. Ganss, S.J. (New York/Mahwah: Paulist Press, 1991), 241.

4. Martha Zechmeister, IBVM, *Mystik und Sendung* (Würzburg, Echter Verlag, 1985), 100.

Chapter 8

1. *Darkness in the Marketplace* (Notre Dame, Indiana: Ave Maria Press, 1981), 39–53, esp. 48–50.

2. The German expression "Gotteskomplex" comes from Horst E. Richter.

3. This text is from Anthony de Mello, *The song of the Bird*, p. 182f; cf. footnote 1–4. Another version of the same story is given by Rabindranath Tagore in his *Fruit-Gathering*, in: *Collected Poems and Plays of Rabindranath Tagore* (New York: The Macmillan Company, 1967), 149.

Chapter 9

1. I make use of an anonymous meditation, which I once found. Despite considerable efforts, I was not able to trace the author.

2. Bernardin Schellenberger, OCSO, *Nacht leuchtet wie der Tag* (Freiburg-Basel-Wien: Herder, 1981), 12.

Chapter 10

1. Rabindranath Tagore, *Collected Poems*, p. 146; cf. footnote 8–3.

2. Henri J. M. Nouwen, *Lifesigns–Intimacy, Fecundity, and Ecstacy in Christian Perspective* (Garden City, N.Y.: Doubleday, 1986), 65.

3. *De Consideratione*, I, II, 3, PL 182, 730f English Translation: Bernard of Clairvaux, *Five Books on Consideration–Advice to a Pope*, translated by John D. Anderson and Elisabeth T. Kennan (Kalamazoo, MI, Cistercian Publications, 1976), 27–29.

Chapter 11

1. Henri J. M. Nouwen, *The Genesee Diary–Report from a Trappist Monastery* (Garden City, N.Y.: Doubleday, 1976), p. 12 and p. 60.

2. *Schreiben der deutschen Bischöfe über den priesterlichen Dienst*, Sept. 24, 1992, p. 15.

3. *Collected Poems*, p. 141; cf. footnote 8–3.

Chapter 13

1. *Scintillae Ignatianae* (Vienna, 1705); English translation by Alan G. McDougall, *Thoughts of St. Ignatius Loyola for Every Day of the Year* (London: Burn Oates and Washbourne, 1928) p. 1, Jan. 2.

Chapter 14

1. This story may be apocryphal. My attempt to locate it in the Franciscan Sources failed.

Chapter 15

1. Quoted without reference in: Chaim Potok, *The Book of Lights* (New York, Fawcett Crest, 1982), 104.

2. Sermo 52, VI, 16; PL 38, 360.

3. Blessed Elisabeth of the Trinity (†1906) was deeply touched when she discovered her new name in the letter to the Ephesians (1:6, 12, 14). After that time she took delight in calling herself "Laudem Gloriae"–the Praise of His Glory. She really focuses on an essential aspect of our relationship with God.

4. Here once again the text of St. Thérèse Couderc is illustrative (See Appendix.)

Chapter 16

1. *Vielleicht ist irgendwo Tag–Aufzeichnungen* (Freiburg-Heidelberg: F.H. Kerle-Verlag, 1981), 205f.

Chapter 17

1. *The Way of the Pilgrim,* translated from the Russian by R.M. French (New York: Seabury Press, 1974), 31.

2. Wilkie Au, S.J., *By Way of the Heart–Toward a Holistic Christian Spirituality* (New York/Mahwah: Paulist Press, 1989), 90.

3. *Adversus Haereses* IV, 20, 7; PG 7, 1037.

4. *Ibid.* (See footnote 7–3), pp. 260–264.

5. Part III, #288.

Chapter 18

1. A few weeks later, on March 30, 1984, he died in Innsbruck, Austria, after a short illness. The text can be found in: *Herder Korrespondenz* 38/5 (May 1984), 224–230, and will be used several times in the next paragraphs.

2. *Ibid.* (See footnote 16–1), p. 199f.

3. See ch. 21–23 of this book.

Chapter 20

1. Cf. Jean Lafrance, *La Prière du Coeur* (Paris, 1980), 56 and 76.

2. *Markings*, translated by Leif Sjöberg and W. H. Auden (London: Faber and Faber, 1964), 147; italics by Hammarskjöld.

3. Leonardo Boff, *Saint Francis–A Model for Human Liberation* (New York: Crossroad, 1982), 130.

Chapter 21

1. Waltraud Herbstrith, OCD, *Das wahre Gesicht Edith Steins* (Bergen-Enkheim: Verlag Gerhard Kaffke, 1972), 44.

2. Until 1990 this baptism was unknown except to the woman who administered the sacrament. She then revealed her secret. Cf. Jürgen Kuhlmann, "Gültig getauft–Neues über Simone Weil," in *Geist und Leben* 63 (1990), 39–42.

3. Frankfurtam Main, Josef Knecht, 1957.

Chapter 24

1. I elaborate here on some thoughts which I presented more briefly in an article on the "Examination of Conscience," *Review for Religious*, 1990, 604–609.

2. March 18, 1542: M.I.I. Epist. I, 192f. English translation in William J. Young, S.J., *Letters of St. Ignatius of Loyola* (Chicago: Loyola University Press, 1959), 55.

Chapter 25

1. *St. Francis of Assisi*, (London: Hodder, 1960), 92f.

2. *Wellsprings* (Anand, India: Gujarat Sahitya Prakash, 1984), 26.

3. *Geist und leben* 29 (1956), 289.

4. In his lengthy letter to Sor Teresa Rejadella, OSB, of June 18, 1536, Ignatius teaches her to overcome false humility: "If you reflect, you will realize that these desires to serve Christ our Lord do not come from yourself but are given to you by the Lord. And so when you say, 'The Lord gives me strong desires to serve him," it is the Lord himself you are praising by making known his gift; it is he and not yourself in whom you boast, since you do not attribute the grace to yourself." See: *Ignatius of Loyola* p. 334 (cf footnote 7–3).

5. *De Beneficiis* III,1.